George B. Hartzog, Jr.

*A Great Director
of the
National Park Service*

A Festschrift

George B. Hartzog, Jr. enjoying his favorite pastime. Photo taken after 1972.
National Park Service Historic Photograph Collection, Harpers Ferry Center.

George B. Hartzog, Jr.

A Great Director of the National Park Service

A Festschrift

Edited by Frank P. Sherwood

Every effort has been made to trace all copyright-holders, but if any have been inadvertently overlooked, the publisher will be pleased to make the necessary arrangement at the first opportunity.

Copyright 2011 by Clemson University
ISBN: 978-0-9835339-1-7

Published by Clemson University Press in Clemson, South Carolina.

Editorial Assistants: Christina Cook

To order copies, please visit the Clemson University Press website: www.clemson.edu/press

Cover photo: George Hartzog at Yellowstone, 1972, by Cecil W. Stoughton, courtesy of the National Park Service Historic Photograph Collection, Harpers Ferry Center.

Cover landscape photo: Denali National Park, courtesy of the National Park Service.

Cover design by Christina Cook.

Contents

Preface
    by Lawrence R. Allen with assistance from Frank P. Sherwood................... vi

Acknowledgments xiii

Chapter One

His Boss for Five Years Reflects on George B. Hartzog, Jr., from the "Introduction" to *Battling for the National Parks*
    by Stewart L. Udall 1

Chapter Two

The Details of the National Parks Expansion in the Hartzog Years: 1964–1972
    by Barry Mackintosh and Frank P. Sherwood 5

Chapter Three

George B. Hartzog, Jr. : The Man and the Mission
    by Frank P. Sherwood 29

Chapter Four

George B. Hartzog, Jr. : Leader—Executive—Manager
    by Frank P. Sherwood 69

Notes on Contributors 108

Preface

The name George B. Hartzog, Jr. occupies a major place in the Clemson University pantheon of special people. The relationship with George and Helen Hartzog was fostered by William C. Everhart and his wife, Mary, who wanted to honor the man who they considered the pre-eminent director of the National Park Service. Everhart served as Assistant Director under George, and, in 1978, he served as a Visiting Professor at Clemson where he established the Hartzog Fund. Out of this initial gift grew the Hartzog Lecture Series and the George B. Hartzog, Jr. Environmental Awards. While George was still in good health, he and Helen would attend the Lecture Series each year that honored a distinguished leader in environmental management and stewardship. This program continues today at Clemson University where it attracts an international audience and now presents six different environmental awards to acclaimed leaders and researchers.

And finally, Hartzog's voluminous papers, particularly covering the eventful years when he was Director of the National Park Service, are held in Clemson University libraries. Thus, Hartzog's legacy at Clemson is not only conceptual but is also, in a very marked way, tangible.

It is also noteworthy that George B. Hartzog, Jr. was a true South Carolinian. He was born in 1920 in Walterboro, South Carolina, and spent virtually all his years there until he entered the Army in 1943. While he lived elsewhere throughout the rest of his career, his final resting place was with his family in Walterboro. He died at age eighty-eight in 2008. Given this kind of background, it is not surprising that this book on Hartzog's life and work is being published by the Clemson University Digital Press.

This is a book about a man who may have done more to give the parks their present character than anyone in their history. Therefore we have titled our volume *George B. Hartzog, Jr.: A Great Director of the National Park Service* because that is certainly what he was. While Stephen T. Mather, the founder of the Park system and its director for the first twelve years, will always be recognized as a sainted figure in Park Service annals, the only person who might rival him is Hartzog.

Hartzog was one of the longest serving of the NPS Directors. Mather leads the list—but only barely. Two Directors, Newton Drury and Conrad Wirth (Hartzog's immediate predecessor) logged in slightly over eleven years. Hartzog's nearly nine years places him fourth; and none of the eleven people who have followed him have been in office nearly so long.

Dry statistics do not, however, provide justification for a book. The nine Hartzog years constituted a time of growth, creativity, and real excitement. This book, though relatively short, seeks to capture at least a portion of the exhilaration that Hartzog's inspired leadership provided.

First, the book must provide evidence that Hartzog was a highly successful and effective leader of the parks. That is our purpose in the first two chapters. Second, it must impart profound insights into the spirit, character, values and behavior of a person whom many regard as truly remarkable. That is the goal of Frank Sherwood in the essays he has written that comprise Chapters 3 and 4. Hartzog's accomplishments in the Park Service could easily fill a very long book. It has required great discipline, then, to restrict Chapters 1 and 2 to a relatively few pages.

At the outset, it was important to discover a source that could provide assurance that Hartzog was a person who really did make a difference in the parks. We were very lucky in this regard. Stewart Udall was appointed Secretary of the Interior by John F. Kennedy and served throughout the Kennedy administration and also that of Lyndon B. Johnson, logging a total of eight years in the role. For five of them, he was George Hartzog's boss. While there were the typical intervening layers of bureaucracy, the fact was that the two men were in heavy interaction throughout the period. Udall knew Hartzog well and had a fine opportunity to judge his performance on the job.

But that is not the whole story. Udall had a big investment in Hartzog. As will be discovered later in this book, it was Udall who skipped over a number of more senior people to appoint Hartzog Director in 1964. Indeed, when he discovered that Hartzog had resigned from the Service because he saw no opportunities ahead, it was Udall who sought him out in St. Louis and offered him the Directorship.

How did Udall become so conscious of this highly promising young man? To be sure, part of his awareness came from Hartzog's distinguished record, particularly at the Jefferson National Expansion Memorial (the Gateway Arch). Beyond that, however, there was interpersonal chemistry. Udall describes the circumstance of their first encounter on the Current River in the Ozarks in Chapter 1. He observed that the experience "… established a rapport between me and George B. Hartzog that opened a door to the remarkable public career described in the book."[1] Particularly fascinating are three aspects of this encounter: first, this was in substantial degree a one-on-one relationship; second, it was Hartzog who had the data, the ideas, and the plans to create a unique national park facility; and third, this was an involvement that lay totally outside his basic areas of responsibility. (Hartzog worked on the project largely on weekends and in the evenings.)

Thus, Udall and Hartzog (who were almost exactly the same age) had a working relationship that must be judged unique in any large organization and exceptional in the Federal government. It was fortunate that Udall agreed to write the Introduction to Hartzog's book *Battling for the National Parks*, published in 1988, as it provides a very insightful examination of the Hartzog performance as Director of the National Park Service. Udall begins by declaring, "George Hartzog was one of the most inspiring leaders I worked with during my years in the Federal government."[2] There is much in this book reporting other evaluations, but the one from Udall stands out as a true certification of Hartzog's impressive qualities as a leader.

While there are many ways in which the Hartzog performance might be evaluated in a more factual, quantitative form, certainly one is the size of the enterprise at the beginning of the tenure and at the end. On this criterion, Hartzog cannot be compared. During his nine years in office, he was directly responsible for adding 69 units to the parks system. That is a record for the tenure of any Director. It was nearly three-quarters as many additions as had occurred in the prior thirty years (1933–1963) under four Directors. And it was only four short of the increase recorded in the eleven years after his departure (1973–1984) under three Directors.

Though he was no longer the Director, Hartzog is regarded as having had a major hand in the greatest expansion in the history of the Park Service, the doubling of lands with acquisitions in Alaska. The story of how that approval process was initiated in 1970 by Hartzog against tremendous opposition is intimately recorded in Chapter XVI, "Alaska," of Hartzog's book.[3]

Significantly, the specifics of the expansion of the parks under Hartzog were carefully detailed in a publication of the National Park Service, *The National Parks: Shaping the System*.[4] This book covers the ground so beautifully that we had only to excerpt parts of it for inclusion in our volume.

Thus, a small book published more than twenty-five years ago has made the production of this volume much easier. In fact, however, our debt to the Park Service goes beyond this single case. In 2005, the Service issued a publication, *Oral History Interview with George B. Hartzog, Jr.*, which gave him an opportunity to reflect on the near decade of leadership experience he had about thirty-five years earlier.[5] It is a rich source of insight about the Hartzog years and one which Frank Sherwood drew on heavily in writing Chapter 4 on the man as leader, executive, and manager. This Park Service publication did much to make Sherwood's chapter richer. And it causes me to emphasize again how great is our debt to the National Park Service for the extreme care and attention to quality it has pursued in making its history available to the public.

In the first of his two essays, which constitute a major part of this book, Sherwood seeks to capture at least a portion of the excitement experienced during the nine years of Hartzog's leadership of the parks. However, it is important to understand that Sherwood wrote roughly twenty years after Hartzog's departure from office. His purpose in writing was to include Hartzog in a book on "exemplars" in American public administration. The essay appeared in 1992 in *Exemplary Public Administrators: Character and Leadership in Government*.[6] The present chapter is a revision and expansion of the original, completed roughly another two decades later.

There are three main sections of the chapter. The first seeks further to establish Hartzog's credentials as a highly successful leader. It builds on earlier chapters by reporting other sources from which highly positive evaluations of Hartzog have come. The second section is perhaps the most significant, providing a picture of the way in which this charismatic man operated in the Park Service. The third section provides an insight into a public service career that we seldom see. Hartzog's strong leadership produced enemies, well beyond President Nixon, and they appeared at his retirement. He spent his first five years out of office defending himself against a wide array of charges. It required large amounts of time and considerable sums of money. In the end none of the charges stuck. Hartzog retained his reputation as a person of complete integrity.

Certainly Sherwood's job of portraying George Hartzog in motion was made easier by the availability of some truly remarkable resources. The first was a highly revealing profile of George Hartzog, written by a very accomplished writer, John McPhee, that appeared in *The New Yorker* magazine September 11, 1971.[7] Not only has it been rare for *The New Yorker* to devote its treasured space to a government bureaucrat, but the essay itself was very lengthy. Clearly, McPhee became heavily involved with Hartzog and used his great talents to provide an intimate, close-up view of this unique person. Sherwood refers frequently to the article in his writing.

Hartzog's own book, *Battling for the National Parks,* was far more important than most autobiographical works by public figures.[8] It engages in full disclosure. There is nothing Hartzog is unwilling to reveal, and anyone seeking to understand the interface of bureaucracy and politics can find no better source. Furthermore, it is a pleasure to read. Sherwood places heavy reliance on it.

Finally, there was the substantial output on the National Park Service by Hartzog's old friend and associate, Bill Everhart. Bill provides a further independent perspective on much that went on in these important years as he shared many experiences with his boss during their tenure together.

Sherwood's second chapter (Chapter 4) is quite different from the preceding one. It was written after Hartzog's death and completed in 2010. Thus, it reflects on a career that was at its peak forty years earlier. Hartzog is seen as a very old man, and Sherwood undertakes to describe those traits he saw continuing to persist and speculates on their presence and relevance at an earlier time in Hartzog's life.

Most of the chapter, however, is devoted to a description of the personal style and behaviors that permit us to characterize George Hartzog as a leader, an executive, and a manager. This is an academic area, incidentally, where Sherwood boasts significant expertise. Not only was he the first Director of the Federal Executive Institute, but much of his research and teaching has been concerned with leaders in government—their roles, interactions, and behaviors. There is a typology in this literature which places emphasis on three constructs: (a) the leader, which is a more general designation for people carrying a common responsibility to assemble and propel a group of people toward a common objective; (b) the executive, which is applied more selectively to the very few at the hierarchical top of an organization who have the legitimacy to set the terms of behavior and the directions for an undertaking; and (c) the manager, which is used more broadly for all those who have the capacity and the responsibility to influence at least pieces of an organization. The application of the latter term is broad, covering all those engaged in management. Clearly, George Hartzog belonged in all three of these categories. His leadership was not something reserved to a specific activity but was characteristic of George Hartzog at large. It permeated his very being.

On the other hand, his categorization as an executive related specifically to his service as Director of the National Park Service. The Directorship made him the formal head of the 13,000 people then comprising the Service. While according him certain command prerogatives, it most significantly bestowed a major responsibility on him, namely to maintain the Park Service as a viable entity and to guide it to improved performance as the custodian of the nation's parks. This responsibility's weight was strongly reflected in one of the questions Hartzog asked in his book: "Whose parks are these?" This duty also required that Hartzog live in many different worlds—all outside the NPS itself—in order to represent, assert, and defend the interests of his organization.

The burdens of the executive have appeared so great to many observers that personal time emerges as the most prized resource. An executive, like every other individual, has a limited amount of time available. Therefore, it has been argued that he or she can no longer be involved with affairs inside the organization, that is, with its management. In this theory, the executive can no longer see himself or herself as a manager. It is an idea, however, that George Hartzog rejected completely, though it may have never come to his attention; and it may differentiate him markedly from others in executive roles.

It has to be understood that Hartzog was not only the chief executive of the Park Service but also continued to occupy a key management role. He did not follow the usual path of the executive in leaving the management to others and thus ignored tradition by remaining intimately engaged in the operations of the Service. Sherwood believes that the perception of Hartzog as the manager of the Park Service produced a great benefit. It greatly increased his credibility in the outside world. Those who transacted with the Park Service knew that any promises Hartzog made would be fully honored. He would see that the pledged behaviors occurred.

How did Hartzog operate so successfully in two such demanding roles? The key was his great capacity to delegate significant responsibilities in the management of the Service. It is Sherwood's theory that immense personal confidence enabled Hartzog to trust himself, with the further consequence that he could place his full trust in others. Thus, he was a master delegator, reserving for himself involvement only in those areas he deemed too important to leave to others.

In conclusion, Sherwood expresses his deep regret that the personal animosity of a president (Richard Nixon), who apparently developed without any real exposure to Hartzog, deprived the nation of a superb leader of its parks long before his time should have ended. Hartzog was only fifty-four, at the peak of his capacities, when the dismissal occurred. Sherwood believes that he might well have guided the parks for another ten years—until a time when he might normally have retired. He asks how the parks might have fared with Hartzog at the helm for another decade.

As Frank Sherwood confesses, there is so much in the large Hartzog arsenal of assets that it is difficult to identify a very few attributes that made him special. However, Sherwood sees Hartzog's desire for further learning and growth as possibly his single greatest asset. While this zest for continued improvement was an important personal incentive, the crucial point is that Hartzog saw it as the means by which he could realize the full potential of his endeavors within the park service.

Lawrence R. Allen, with assistance from Frank P. Sherwood, Clemson, SC

Notes

1. George B. Hartzog, Jr., *Battling for the National Parks*. Mt. Kisco, New York; Moyer Bell Limited, 1988, xii
2. Hartzog, xi.
3. Ibid., 203–223
4. *The National Parks: Shaping the System*. Washington, DC : Division of Publications, National Park Service, 1985. 112 pp., paper.
5. *Oral History Interview with George B. Hartzog, Jr*. Washington, DC: Park History Program, National Park Service, 2005.
6. Terry Cooper and N. Dale Wright, *Exemplary Public Administrators: Character and Leadership in Government*. (San Francisco: Jossey-Bass, 1992), 139–165.
7. John McPhee, "Profile: G. Hartzog," New Yorker. 45: 48 (September 11, 1971)
8. Hartzog, *op. cit.*

Acknowledgments

Special thanks go to Jonathan B. Jarvis, Director of the National Park Service, for advice to the editor, his assistant, and the publisher on proper use of the NPS document entitled *The National Parks: Shaping the System*, a publication instrumental to the creation of this timely tribute to George B. Hertzog, Jr. Thanks to Senator Tom Udall's office and Helen Hartzog for guiding our use of excerpts from Hartzog's memoir, *Battling for the National Parks*, including a short tribute by the late Stewart Udall, Secretary of the U.S. Department of the Interior from 1961 to 1969. We are grateful, also, to Stacy Mason of the Harpers Ferry Center for assisting us in procuring high-resolution cover images and advising us on the use of images from NPS archives.

Further appreciation goes to Lawrence R. Allen and the College of Health, Education, and Human Development, Clemson University, for underwriting the cost of production and for bringing this fine work to our attention in the first place. Thanks to Frank P. Sherwood for working with us to bring his vision to fruition. Many thanks, too, to Christina Cook in her role as textual and graphic designer of this book. Her beautiful cover design speaks for itself even if her documentary sleuthing on behalf of the editor and her many incremental improvements are invisible to the reader, as is generally true of the endeavor to articulate a unified chorale from several voices. In the way of definition, one might add that *festschriften* are volumes comprised of writings by various persons assembled with the common aim of paying tribute to, or memorializing, an admired associate.

Much of the work appearing in this book derives from sources now in public domain, but every effort has been made to trace all copyright-holders. If any have been overlooked, the publisher will be pleased to make the necessary arrangement at the first opportunity.

Wayne K. Chapman
Executive Editor
Clemson University Digital Press

From left to right: Conrad L Wirth, Secretary Stewart L. Udall, A. Clark Stratton, and George B. Hartzog, Jr., as Hartzog is sworn in as Director, 1964. National Park Service Historic Photograph Collection, Harpers Ferry Center.

Chapter One

HIS BOSS FOR FIVE YEARS REFLECTS ON GEORGE B. HARTZOG, JR., FROM THE "INTRODUCTION" TO BATTLING FOR THE NATIONAL PARKS [1]

by Stewart L. Udall [2]

George Hartzog was one of the most inspiring leaders I worked with during my years in the Federal government, so it gives me immense pleasure to pen an introduction to this memoir. Indeed, part of that pleasure derives from the circumstance that I had the gumption, after one of our reminiscing visits two years ago, to "demand" that he owed it to history and to his friends to write an account of his adventures in public service.

George has neglected to relate how he grabbed the "brass ring" that opened the door to the office of the Director of the National Park Service, so I will fill in that gap in his narrative. On becoming Secretary of the Interior, I made it a practice to inspect proposed new additions to the National Park System—and in the fall of 1961 I found myself floating on the Current River in the Ozarks with an exuberant group of Missouri conservationists, who were mounting a campaign to preserve some of their state's finest free-flowing rivers.

As Park Superintendent of the Jefferson National Expansion Memorial at St. Louis, Hartzog had volunteered to work out the itinerary for this outing and; as I soon learned, had already formulated a political game-plan to turn the "Show Me" State's rivers into a new kind of national park. George explained the elements of his plan while we were enroute [sic] to the Ozarks. He shrewdly analyzed the controversies that were swirling around this project; he provided vivid descriptions of the proponents and opponents; he offered insights about Ozark folkways; and he even ventured to tell me how I should "play my cards" to disarm the anti-biases of the "hillbillies" who lived along these rivers.

Our two-day tour to publicize the potential of the proposed park was, on several counts, a huge success: it paved the way for the creation of the nation's first national rivers parkland in 1964; it gave me invaluable insights into the art of marshalling local and national support for additions to the National Park system; and, not least, it established a rapport between me and George B. Hartzog that opened a door to the extraordinary public career described in this book.

Beyond his skill as a park planner, it was the winning, masterful touch George had in dealing with all kinds of people that made him an unforgettable person. From that first encounter there was a brotherly relationship between us; we were the same age, and we had both learned about life growing up during the Great Depression in small towns (he in rural South Carolina, myself in Arizona's high country).

As you read on, you will be delighted to discover that, although by present-day standards George had few formal educational opportunities, he learned enough by dint of what passed for self-improvement in those days to be ordained as a Methodist minister at 17, to acquire enough shorthand to be a court reporter at 18, and to "read" enough law to pass the South Carolina bar exam on his third try without attending a school of law.

In any event, indelible impressions of a man named George Hartzog were imbedded in my mind when Conrad Wirth decided in 1962 to retire as director, just as we were gearing up for what would become the largest expansion of the National Park System in our nation's history. There was a twinge of anguish among the old guard in the Park Service when it became known that I favored a generational leadership change and had selected George Hartzog as the new Director. But I wanted a new dynamism—and I now believe that evidence adduced in this book vindicates the choice I made.

This book both documents the dynamism generated by Director Hartzog, and includes enough "combat stories" to inform us how George tackled some of the problems he encountered during his days in the Park Service. George is a wonderful storyteller, and we are fortunate that his editor lets his voice speak to us in the exact inflections he uses in everyday conversation. To read this book is to know a man.

In a decade when a President of the United States seeks out opportunities to denigrate the institution we call the Federal government and belittle the work of its dedicated civil servants, we need antidotes like this book. George Hartzog's story reminds us of the glories of public service and the legacies our best bureaucrats leave to future generations.

George does not draw large conclusions about the outcome of his endeavors, but we who collaborated with him can perform that function. Everyone who saw him in action or who entered what he called his "command post" at the National Park Service remembers the sense of mission and the zest and drive he transmitted to his co-workers. Hartzog, as some of the episodes he cites attest, was a consummate negotiator: he enjoyed entering political thickets, and he had the self-confidence and savvy to be his own lobbyist and to win most of his arguments with members of Congress, Governors, and Presidents.

And George, as his words demonstrate on every page, was always the happy warrior who exuded reasonableness and good will. His signature was the greeting he invariably extended to ordinary citizens and Senators alike: "Hello my friend, what can I do for you?" As an administrator, he set an exemplary standard for commitment, for candor, and for fair play.

Notes

1. Stewart L. Udall, the Secretary of the Interior for eight years, from 1961 to 1969, directly supervised Hartzog from 1964 to 1969.
2. Stewart L. Udall, "Introduction," *Battling for the National Parks*, by George B. Hartzog, Jr. (Mt. Kisco, NY: Moyer Bell, Ltd., 1988), xi-xiii.

George Hartzog as Assistant Superintendant of Rocky Mountain National Park, 1956. Photo by R. Taylor. National Park Service Historic Photograph Collection, Harpers Ferry Center.

Chapter Two

THE DETAILS OF THE NATIONAL PARKS EXPANSION IN THE HARTZOG YEARS: 1964–72

EDITOR'S NOTE:

In 1984 the National Park Service published a small book, *The National Parks: Shaping the System*. It undertakes to describe the evolution of the National Park system, which it identified as the first of its kind in the world. Though he is not given credit for the book, Barry Mackintosh, the Park Service historian, wrote the critical, highly detailed section on the way in which the park system evolved. The only phase of development which was identified by the name of the Director was 1964–1972, labeled "The Hartzog Years." Mackintosh amply demonstrates the remarkable contribution Hartzog made to the expansion of the parks.

—Frank P. Sherwood

PART I: "THE HARTZOG YEARS, 1964 TO 1972"

by Barry Mackintosh[1]

The nine years from 1964 through 1972 began with the formal administrative division of the National Park System into natural, historical, and recreational area categories and concluded with the centennial observance of the first national park, Yellowstone. Sixty-nine of the 334 units present in 1984 were authorized or acquired during these nine years—nearly three-quarters as many as had been permanently added in the preceding 30 years. The Director during these years was George B. Hartzog, Jr., who came to the office at a favorable time. Mission 66, the 10-year program of upgrading the parks, was coming to an end. Stewart L. Udall, Secretary of the Interior, found in Hartzog a willing ally who would push Udall's expansionist and activist park policy for President Lyndon B. Johnson's "Great Society." Backed by a rejuvenated system and his Secretary's support, Hartzog was set to put his imprint upon the Service.

On July 10, 1964, Secretary Udall signed a key management policy memorandum based on recommendations from Director Hartzog."In looking back at the legislative enactments that have shaped the National Park System," it said, "it is clear that the Congress has included within the growing system three different categories of areas—natural, historical, and recreational. Each of these categories requires a separate management concept and a separate set of management principles coordinated to form one organic management plan for the entire system." Natural areas were to be managed for perpetuation and restoration of their natural values, although significant historic features within a natural area should be maintained "to the extent compatible with the primary purpose for which the area was established." In historical areas these emphases were reversed. In recreational areas, both natural and historic resource preservation would be subordinate to management for outdoor recreation. Use of such areas would focus on "active participation in outdoor recreation in a pleasing environment."

At the time, as was noted in the last chapter, most areas assigned to the recreational category were technically excluded from the National Park System by the legal definition of 1953. That law reflected concern that if reservoirs and other artificially developed recreation facilities were admitted anywhere in the System, they would degrade it and might soon invade the traditional parks as well. The Udall policy memorandum seemingly violated the 1953 law by granting system membership to such areas, but it allayed concern that they might taint the natural parks by placing them in a distinct subclass with distinct management policies. Separate policy manuals were developed for the three area categories and appeared in 1968. Two years later law caught up with administrative initiative when Congress redefined the system to include all areas administered "for park, monument, historic, parkway, recreational, or other purposes" by the National Park Service.

The Udall memorandum also prescribed a Service objective "to develop the National Park System through inclusion of additional areas of scenic, scientific, historical and recreational value to the Nation." This perennial mission of the Bureau, expansionist from its beginnings, was reiterated in the Service policy memorandum signed June 18, 1969, by Udall's successor, Secretary Walter J. Hickel: "The National Park System should protect and exhibit the best examples of our great national landscapes, riverscapes and shores and undersea environments; the processes which formed them; the life communities that grow and dwell therein; and the important landmarks of our history. There are serious gaps and inadequacies which must be remedied while opportunities still exist if the System is to fulfill the people's need always to see and understand their heritage of history and the natural world. (sic)

"You should continue your studies to identify gaps in the System and recommend to me areas that would fill them. It is my hope that we can make a significant contribution to rounding out more of the National Park System in these next few years."

With this charge in hand, Hartzog ordered preparation of a National Park System Plan, published in 1972. The history component of the Plan employed a modified version of the theme structure used in studies for identifying national historic landmarks. Historical parks were assigned to the various thematic elements, revealing gaps wherever the elements were unrepresented in the System. Developed to provide the greatest possible rationale for expansion, the history component determined that at least 196 new parks were needed to treat fully all major facets of American history and prehistory. The natural history component of the Plan, taking a similar approach, identified more than 300 aspects of natural history requiring initial or greater representation in the System.

Although recreational areas did not lend themselves to the same kind of thematic analysis and were not addressed in the Plan, interest in them did not wane. Their number doubled from 1964 to 1972. Of the 69 new and permanent additions during the Hartzog administration, 27 were classed as recreational—three times as many as the 9 new natural areas and not far behind the 33 new historical units.

Natural Areas

Of the 10 natural areas added during the period, one was later incorporated in an existing national park, leaving nine remaining in today's System. Five of these were new national parks. This notable achievement would not have happened without vigorous efforts by the Service going back many years, newly awakened public and congressional interest, and financial support stemming from the Land and Water Conservation Fund Act of 1965. As amended in 1968, the act earmarked revenues from visitor fees, surplus property sales, motorboat fuel taxes, and offshore oil and gas leasing for Federal and state parkland acquisition.

Canyonlands National Park was established in 1964 to protect a wild area of exceptional scenic, scientific, and archeological importance at the confluence of the Green and Colorado rivers in southeastern Utah. In 1971 President Richard M. Nixon approved legislation adding substantial public land to Canyonlands, bringing the park's total area to more than 337,000 acres.

Congress authorized Guadalupe Mountains National Park in 1966 to preserve an area in west Texas "... possessing outstanding geological values together with scenic and other natural values of great significance." Proposed for inclusion in the system as early as 1933, the park's mountain mass and adjoining lands cover more than 76,000 acres and include portions of the world's most extensive Permian limestone fossil reef.

North Cascades National Park, Washington, embraces 504,780 acres of wild' alpine country with jagged peaks, mountain lakes, and glaciers. From the start this undertaking was surrounded by intense controversy involving timber and mining interests, conservationists, local governments, and several Federal bureaus including the Forest Service, the Bureau of Outdoor Recreation, and the Park Service. The park was finally authorized in 1968 simultaneously with Redwood National Park, California. Redwood, which also followed long and bitter controversy, was intended "... to preserve significant examples of the primeval coastal redwood forests and the streams and seashores with which they are associated for purposes of public inspiration, enjoyment and scientific study." Within its legislated boundaries, enlarged in 1978 to encompass 109,000 acres, are three California state parks dating from the 1920s, 30 miles of Pacific coastline, and the world's tallest trees.

The last new national park of the period was Voyageurs, on the northern edge of Minnesota, authorized in 1971 to preserve the "... scenery, geological conditions, and waterway system which constituted a part of the historic route of the Voyageurs who contributed significantly to the opening of the Northwestern United States." It occupies some 220,000 acres of remote northern lake country.

Besides the five new national parks, two former national monuments, Arches and Capitol Reef in Utah, were upgraded to national park status by legislation in 1971, and a new national monument, Biscayne in the upper Florida keys, formed the basis for Biscayne National Park in 1980. Three other new monuments—Agate Fossil Beds, Nebraska; Florissant Fossil Beds, Colorado; and Fossil Butte, Wyoming—were authorized by acts of Congress to preserve outstanding deposits of mammal, insect, and fish fossils. The fifth new monument, Marble Canyon, was proclaimed by President Johnson to protect the 50-mile canyon of the Colorado River between Grand Canyon National Park and Glen Canyon National Recreation Area. Grand Canyon National Park was enlarged to encompass the monument in 1975.

Of great importance to natural preservation in the system during and after this period was the Wilderness Act of September 3, 1964. It read in part: "In order to assure that an increasing population, accompanied by expanding settlement and growing mechanization, does not occupy and modify all areas within the United States and its possessions, leaving no lands designated for preservation and protection in their natural condition, it is hereby declared to be the policy of the Congress to secure for the American people of present and future generations the benefits of an enduring resource of wilderness. For this purpose there is hereby established a National Wilderness Preservation System to be composed of Federally owned areas designated by Congress as 'wilderness areas', and these shall be administered for the use and enjoyment of the American people in such manner as will leave them unimpaired for future use and enjoyment as wilderness."

The act defined wilderness as "… an area where the earth and its community of life are untrammeled by man, where man himself is a visitor who does not remain." For designation as wilderness an area was to be without permanent improvements or human habitation, to retain "its primeval character and influence," and generally to contain at least 5,000 acres. Among other provisions, the act directed the Secretary of the Interior to review within 10 years every roadless area of 5,000 acres or more in the National Park Service and report to the President on the suitability of each for preservation as wilderness. The President would then report his recommendations to Congress for action.

Although many portions of the system were clearly wilderness and had long been managed as such, the act forced a careful examination of all potentially qualifying lands and consideration as to which should be perpetuated indefinitely without roads, use or motorized equipment, structures, or other development incompatible with formal wilderness designation. By 1972, many areas had been studied and two—in Petrified Forest National Park and Craters of the Moon National Monument—had been confirmed as wilderness by Congress.

HISTORICAL AREAS

Historical additions again led the other categories, with 35 new or essentially new arrivals in the years 1964–1972. Two—Mar-A-Largo National Historic Site and the National Visitor Center—were subsequently dropped from the system, leaving 33 from the period with us today.

Nearly a quarter of the new historical areas were presidential sites. The first, Herbert Hoover National Historic Site in 1965, commemorated Hoover at his birthplace, childhood home, and burial place in West Branch, Iowa. In 1966 the Ansley Wilcox House in Buffalo, New York, where Theodore Roosevelt became President after William McKinley's assassination, was added to the System, becoming known as Theodore Roosevelt Inaugural National Historic Site. The Roosevelt memorial on Theodore Roosevelt Island in Washington, D. C. was dedicated a year later. In 1967 Dwight D. Eisenhower saw his last residence and farm at Gettysburg, Pennsylvania, designated a national historic site, and his successor, John F. Kennedy, was recognized by a national historic site at his Brookline, Massachusetts, birthplace and first residence. William Howard Taft National Historic Site, containing the Cincinnati birthplace and boyhood home of that President, and the Lyndon B. Johnson National Historic Site, ultimately comprising Johnson's birthplace, boyhood home, grandfather's ranch, and LBJ Ranch in Blanco and Gillespie counties, Texas, were both authorized on December 2, 1969. Finally, the property most illustrative of Abraham Lincoln's pre-presidential career, his residence in Springfield, Illinois, became the Lincoln Home National Historic Site in 1972.

This fifth Lincoln site brought him to a tie with Theodore Roosevelt as the most commemorated President in the National Park System.

Although the period saw a moratorium on new battlefield parks, other military history additions continued. Two frontier army posts, Fort Bowie, Arizona, and Fort Larned, Kansas, became national historic sites in 1964. Congress authorized Fort Scott Historic Area, Kansas, a year later as a cooperative venture outside the system, with the Service assisting local jurisdictions and owners in marking and developing the Fort and nearby historic properties. In 1978 Fort Scott was re-designated a national historic site and came under Service administration. George Rogers Clark National Historical Park, 1966, in Vincennes, Indiana, centered on an existing memorial commemorating Clark's victory over the British in 1779, which bolstered America's claim to the Old Northwest. In 1970 came Fort Point

National Historic Site, encompassing a major coastal fortification of the mid-19th century at San Francisco, and Andersonville National Historic Site, containing the notorious Civil War prison camp in Georgia. One of the last acquisitions of the period was an unassuming Philadelphia boardinghouse that became Thaddeus Kosciuszko National Memorial in 1972 to honor the Polish military engineer who served in the American Revolution and briefly occupied the property later.

Along with the growth in these and other well-represented themes, a few areas treating some previously unrepresented and poorly represented subjects also were acquired. The homes of three figures important in American literature—John Muir, Carl Sandburg, and Henry Wadsworth Longfellow—were recognized as national historic sites. The American sculptor Augustus Saint-Gaudens was similarly honored. A national memorial was authorized for Roger Williams, founder of Rhode Island and a pioneer in religious freedom. The System's coverage of industry and transportation was strengthened with the addition of Allegheny Portage Railroad National Historic Site, containing the remains of an inclined plane railroad over the mountains in Pennsylvania; Saugus Iron Works National Historic Site, a reconstructed 17th century industrial complex in Massachusetts; and the Chesapeake and Ohio Canal National Historical Park, a major expansion of the existing national monument to encompass significant lands on the north bank of the Potomac River. Another facet of economic and social history was addressed by Grant-Kohrs Ranch National Historic Site, Montana, containing part of one of the largest 19th-century range ranches in the country. Chamizal National Memorial in El Paso, Texas, was established to commemorate the peaceful settlement of a U. S.-Mexico border dispute.

Another general enactment of the period, the National Historic Preservation Act of October 15, 1966, was of comparable importance to the 1906 Antiquities Act and the 1935 Historic Sites Act in expanding National Park Service preservation activity. Although most of its influence would be felt outside the National Park System, it had major implications within. All historical parks were entered in the National Register of Historic Places authorized by the act, which made Service and other Federal agency actions affecting them subject to evaluation and review by state historic preservation officers and the Advisory Council on Historic Preservation, a new Federal agency established by the act. Under a 1971 executive order and a later amendment to the act, the Service also was required to nominate to the National Register all qualifying historic sites and structures in its natural and recreational areas. These resources, most of local or regional significance, were then afforded the same consideration as the historical parks when faced with potentially adverse actions. The effect was to broaden the Service's concern for all its cultural properties, including those that had previously received little attention.

Recreational Areas

Twenty-seven new areas were assigned to the recreational category in the years 1964 through 1972, a remarkable average of three per year. Nearly half were national seashores and reservoir-related areas in the tradition of those added before, and there was one more parkway. The others were new kinds of areas: national lakeshores, rivers, performing arts facilities, a trail, and two major urban recreation complexes.

The accelerated increase in recreational areas in the System during the period resulted from several factors, including groundwork laid by the Service in earlier surveys, establishment of the Land and Water Conservation Fund, and greater pressures and support for Federal involvement in outdoor recreation during the Kennedy and Johnson administrations. In 1963 the recently formed Recreation Advisory Council, composed of six cabinet-level officials, had proposed a system of national recreation areas and set criteria for them. They were to be spacious, generally including at least 20,000 acres of land and water. They were to be within 250 miles of urban population centers and designed to achieve high recreation carrying capacities, with outdoor recreation opportunities significant enough to attract interstate patronage. Their natural endowments should be "… well above the ordinary in quality and recreation appeal, being of lesser significance than the unique scenic and historic elements of the National Park System, but affording a quality of recreation experience which transcends that normally associated with areas provided by State and local governments." The scale of investment and development should be sufficiently high to warrant Federal involvement. Cooperative management arrangements with the Forest Service, the U. S. Army Corps of Engineers, and possibly other Federal bureaus were expected, with the Park Service playing a leading role at certain areas.

The recreational area category formally adopted by the Park Service in 1964 partially reflected the Recreation Advisory Council's criteria, although not all Park System units that the Service assigned to the category were of the type envisioned by the Council. Several of the national seashores, lakeshores, rivers, and reservoir-based areas most nearly complied with the national recreation area criteria; others were categorized as recreational areas by default because they did not fully accord with the standards and policies for natural or historical areas.

Five new national seashores joined the four previously authorized and the new, but comparable, designation of national lakeshore was applied to four additions on the Great Lakes. The Service had sought preservation of most of these areas since the mid-1950s, when its seashore surveys were largely completed. The system acquired no further lakeshores and only one more seashore (Canaveral) in the decade after 1972, so this subcategory had evolved to virtually its present extent by the end of the period under consideration.

In most cases establishment of these shoreline reservations forestalled development of residential subdivisions, highways, and commercial facilities and preserved threatened natural and historical features. The areas provided important outdoor recreation opportunities in natural environments without the kind of intensive development for mass recreation typified by Jones Beach, New York.

Fire Island National Seashore, not far east of Jones Beach, protects some 25 miles of largely unspoiled barrier beach 50 miles from downtown Manhattan. Contrary to the Recreation Advisory Council's position that outdoor recreation should be the dominant management purpose in such areas, the seashore's enabling act specified that "... the Secretary [of the Interior] shall administer and protect the Fire Island National Seashore with the primary aim of conserving the natural resources located there."

Assateague Island National Seashore, authorized a year later in 1965, occupies a 35-mile-long barrier island on the Eastern Shore of Maryland and Virginia within reach of the Baltimore and Washington metropolitan areas. Political compromises resulted in joint management by the National Park Service, U. S. Fish and Wildlife Service, and Maryland Park Service. In exchange for local support of the seashore legislation, the Service was legally directed to build a highway and major concessions developments along the island, but conservationists' opposition led to repeal of these provisions in 1976. A new management plan for Assateague emphasizes natural preservation rather than development for mass recreation.

Cape Lookout National Seashore, extending southwest from Cape Hatteras National Seashore on the Outer Banks of North Carolina, was authorized by a 1966 act that repeated the general statement of purpose originally legislated for Assateague: "The Secretary shall administer the… Seashore for the general purposes of public outdoor recreation, including conservation of natural features contributing to public enjoyment." Although conservation was thus subordinated to recreation, Cape Lookout, too, has been lightly developed for recreational use.

Gulf Islands National Seashore, authorized in 1971, came closer than its predecessors to the Council's vision of a national recreation area. The islands in its Mississippi portion, however, accessible only by boat, contained natural and historic features whose preservation was of paramount importance, and a Spanish-American fort near Pensacola, Florida, was a national historic landmark.

The final national seashore of the period, Cumberland Island, Georgia, was least consistent with the recreation area concept. Its 1972 legislation included stringent development restrictions: with certain exceptions, "… the seashore shall be permanently preserved in its primitive state, and no development of the project or plan for the convenience of visitors shall be undertaken which would be incompatible with the preservation of the unique flora and fauna…, nor shall any road or causeway connecting Cumberland Island to the mainland be constructed." It remains among the most "natural" of the seashores.

The four national lakeshores generally followed the seashore pattern. Indiana Dunes, on the southern shore of Lake Michigan between Gary and Michigan City, Indiana, had been proposed as a national park as early as 1917. Although it was the most urban of the four, serving the greater Chicago area, its legislation stressed natural conservation at least as much as recreation. Sleeping Bear Dunes, occupying 34 miles of shoreline on upper Lake Michigan, was to be administered "… in a manner which provides for recreational opportunities consistent with the maximum protection of the natural environment within the area." Pictured Rocks, Michigan, the first of the national lakeshores, and Apostle Islands, Wisconsin, both on the south shore of Lake Superior, also protected resources of great natural and scenic value. Had the laws authorizing most of the seashores and lakeshores not permitted hunting, an activity prohibited in the national parks and monuments, many would have readily fitted the Service's natural area category.

During these years the Service became involved at eight existing or proposed reservoirs. Four of these national recreation areas—Bighorn Canyon, Delaware Water Gap, Lake Chelan, and Ross Lake—were authorized by special acts of Congress; Service responsibilities at the others were set by cooperative agreements with other agencies. Most resembled their predecessors, but Delaware Water Gap, Lake Chelan, and Ross Lake deserve special mention.

Ross Lake and Lake Chelan, Washington, were authorized together in 1968 with the adjacent North Cascades National Park. They were planned as areas in which to concentrate physical development, especially visitor accommodations, outside the national park—the first time a provision of this type was made at the outset in conjunction with park legislation. The Ross Lake area lies between the north and south units of the national park, which is adjoined by Lake Chelan on the southeast. The park and the two national recreation areas collectively embrace more than 684,240 acres of magnificent mountain country in the Cascade Range.

Delaware Water Gap National Recreation Area in Pennsylvania and New Jersey was authorized in 1965 to encompass the proposed Tocks Island Reservoir, a 37-mile-long Corps of Engineers impoundment, and scenic lands in the adjoining Delaware Valley totaling 71,000 acres. The System's first national recreation area east of the Mississippi, it was envisioned to serve 10 million visitors annually from the New York and Philadelphia metropolitan areas. But the Tocks Island Dam came under heavy attack from conservationists and others, especially after the National Environmental Policy Act of 1969 forced greater consideration of the environmental effects of such projects. Without repealing the authorization for the dam, Congress in 1978 ordered the lands acquired by the Corps to be transferred to the Service and made the Delaware River within the recreation area a national scenic river—a designation incompatible with its damming. There is little likelihood that the area will become what was originally planned, at least during this century.

The first of the national rivers and scenic riverways was Ozark National Scenic Riverways in southeastern Missouri, authorized by Congress in 1964 "for the purpose of conserving and interpreting unique scenic and other natural values and objects of historic interest, including preservation of portions of the Current River and the Jacks Fork River in Missouri as free-flowing streams, preservation of springs and caves, management of wildlife, and provisions for use and enjoyment of the outdoor recreation resources thereof by the people of the United States." This linear area incorporated some 140 miles of river and three state parks in its nearly 80,000 acres.

The Ozark authorization was a forerunner of the comprehensive Wild and Scenic Rivers Act of October 2, 1968, which instituted a national wild and scenic rivers system based on conservationust philosophy: "It is hereby declared to be the policy of the United States that certain selected rivers of the Nation, which, with their immediate environments, possess outstandingly remarkable scenic, recreational, geologic, fish and wildlife, historic, cultural, or other similar values, shall be preserved in free-flowing condition, and that they and their immediate environments shall be protected for the benefit and enjoyment of present and future generations. The Congress declares that the established national policy of dams and other construction at appropriate sections of the rivers of the United States needs to be complemented by a policy that would preserve other selected rivers or sections thereof in their free-flowing condition to protect the water quality of such rivers and to fulfill other vital national conservation purposes."

The act identified eight rivers and adjacent lands in nine states as initial components of the national wild and scenic rivers system, to be administered variously by the secretaries of Agriculture and Interior. Twenty-seven others were named to be studied for potential addition to the system. It was anticipated that some of those found eligible would be managed by states and localities. Of the eight initial components only one, St. Croix National Scenic Riverway in Minnesota and Wisconsin, became a unit of the National Park System. Ideal for canoeing, it contains some 200 miles of the St. Croix River and its Namekagon tributary noted for wildness, clear flowing water, and abundant wildlife. All or portions of three of the study areas later joined the Park System: the Lower St. Croix National Scenic Riverway was authorized in 1972, and the Rio Grande Wild and Scenic River and the Upper Delaware Scenic and Recreational River followed together in 1978.

On March 1, 1972, the Yellowstone centennial date, Congress authorized a related addition not proposed in the Wild and Scenic Rivers Act—Buffalo National River, Arkansas. Its 94,146 acres encompass 132 miles of the clear, free-flowing Buffalo, multicolored bluffs, and numerous springs.

On the same day that President Johnson approved the Wild and Scenic Rivers Act, North Cascades and Redwood national parks, and Lake Chelan and Ross Lake national recreation areas, he also signed the National Trails System Act. The act's initial policy statement defined its purpose: "... In order to provide for the ever-increasing outdoor recreation needs of an expanding population and in order to promote public access to, travel within, and enjoyment and appreciation of the open-air, outdoor areas of the Nation, trails should be established *(i)* primarily, near the urban areas of the Nation, and *(ii)* secondarily, within established scenic areas more remotely located. (sic)

"The purpose of this act is to provide the means for attaining these objectives by instituting a national system of recreation and scenic trails."

National recreation trails, accessible to urban areas, would be designated by the Secretary of the Interior or the Secretary of Agriculture according to specified criteria and guidelines; national scenic trails, generally longer and more remote, would be established only by Congress. The act designated two national scenic trails as initial components of the system: the Appalachian Trail, extending from Mount Katahdin, Maine, to Springer Mountain, Georgia; and the Pacific Crest Trail, running from Mexico to Canada along the Cascades, Sierras, and other ranges.

The Pacific Crest Trail was to be administered by the Secretary of Agriculture and the Appalachian Trail by the Secretary of the Interior. The Appalachian Trail was thus brought into the National Park System. Already well established, it had been conceived in 1921 by Benton MacKaye, forester and philosopher, who saw it as the backbone of a primeval environment. Initially four older New England trail systems, including Vermont's Long Trail begun in 1910, were linked to begin the Appalachian Trail. Additions were made farther south, including long sections through national forests in Virginia and North Carolina. The 2,000-mile trail was essentially completed in 1937 when the last short stretch was opened on Maine's Mount Sugarloaf.

An advisory council appointed by the Secretary of the Interior includes representatives of the Appalachian Trail Conference, the 14 States through which the trail passes, other private organizations, and involved Federal agencies. The National Park Service is responsible for protection, development, and maintenance of the trail within Federally administered areas but encourages the states to care for portions outside Federal jurisdiction.

The National Trails System Act ordered 14 other routes to be studied for possible national scenic trail designation. Two were later designated, and four more became national historic trails upon enactment of legislation in 1978. But the Appalachian Trail is the only such entity under Service administration.

The fourth and most recent parkway currently classed as a unit of the system is the John D. Rockefeller, Jr., Memorial Parkway, Wyoming. Authorized August 25, 1972, the 82-mile scenic corridor, which uses existing roads, links West Thumb in Yellowstone and the south entrance of Grand Teton National Park. It commemorates Rockefeller's significant financial support for many parks, including Grand Teton.

Through the civic-mindedness of Catherine Filene Shouse another new type of area was added to the system. She donated part of her Wolf Trap Farm in Fairfax County, Virginia, to the United States so that it might be developed and maintained as a performing arts center in the National Capital area. The Filene Center, an open-sided auditorium, was completed for the first summer season of performances in 1971. Programs then and since have gained a faithful following in the Washington area. The Filene Center was destroyed by fire in 1982 but has been rebuilt. Performances are arranged by the private Wolf Trap Foundation.

The other area intended primarily as a performing arts facility is the John F. Kennedy Center for the Performing Arts in Washington, D. C. The massive structure with its concert hall, opera house, Eisenhower Theater, two smaller theaters, and restaurants was designed by Edward Durrell Stone and opened in 1972. On June 16 of that year a Congressional enactment assigned to the National Park Service "... maintenance, security, information, interpretation, janitorial and all other services necessary to the nonperforming arts functions" of the center, which serves as the national memorial to President Kennedy.

Two other units of the System where the performing arts play major roles, Chamizal National Memorial and Ford's Theatre National Historic Site, have historical commemoration and interpretation as their primary purposes and were each classed as historical areas.

On October 27, 1972, President Nixon signed legislation establishing two areas of great consequence for the system: Gateway National Recreation Area in New York City and nearby New Jersey and Golden Gate National Recreation Area in Marin and San Francisco counties, California. Each contains seacoast beaches, but their proximity to metropolitan New York and San Francisco and the inclusion of other elements make them far more urban in character and patronage than the national seashores previously established.

Gateway encompasses four major units. In Jamaica Bay, the primary aim is conservation of bird life and other natural resources. Elsewhere, at Breezy Point, Staten Island, and Sandy Hook, recreational beach use predominates, although the legislation made special provision for preserving, interpreting, and using the historic sites and structures on Sandy Hook and Staten Island. Sandy Hook's Fort Hancock and the Sandy Hook Proving Grounds were designated a national historic landmark in 1982. As at most of the other recreational areas, hunting is permitted in designated sections. Gateway covers more than 26,000 acres.

Golden Gate was established "to preserve for public use and enjoyment certain areas … possessing outstanding, natural, historic, scenic, and recreational values, and in order to provide for the maintenance of needed recreational open space necessary to urban environment and planning." The park was authorized to contain 72,815 acres by 1984. Much was taken from Army installations no longer needed for military purposes. Besides its ocean beaches, Golden Gate includes a redwood forest, marshes, historic ships of the National Maritime Museum, historic coastal defense works, and Alcatraz Island with the remains of its infamous penitentiary.

Before Gateway and Golden Gate, virtually all the Service's holdings in major urban areas—outside the Washington, D. C., vicinity—had been small historic sites, where the primary concerns were historic preservation and interpretation. These two acquisitions placed the Service squarely in the business of urban mass recreation. This departure was controversial, and attendant major burdens of funding, staffing, and management refocus would not be met without stress in the decade ahead.

NATIONAL PARK SYSTEM ADDITIONS 1964–1972

1964

Aug. 27 Ozark NSR, Mississippi
Aug. 30 Fort Bowie NHS, Arizona
Aug. 31 Allegheny Portage Railroad NHS, Pennsylvania
Aug. 31 Fort Larned NHS, Kansas
Aug. 31 John Muir NHS, California
Aug. 31 Johnstown Flood NMem, Pennsylvania Aug. 31 Saint-Gaudens NHS, New Hampshire
Sept. 11 Fire Island NS, New York
Sept. 12 Canyonlands NP, Utah
Dec. 31 Bighorn Canyon NRA, Wyoming and Montana

1965

Feb. 1 Arbuckle NRA, Oklahoma (incorporated in Chickasaw NRA 1976)
Feb. 11 Curecanti NRA, Colorado
March 15 Sanford NRA, Texas (redesignated Lake Meredith Recreation Area 1972)
May 15 Nez Perce NHP, Idaho
June 5 Agate Fossil Beds NM, Nebraska June 28 Pecos NM, New Mexico
Aug. 12 Herbert Hoover NHS, Iowa
Aug. 28 Hubbell Trading Post NHS, Arizona
Aug. 31 Alibates Flint Quarries and Texas Panhandle Pueblo Culture NM, Texas (redesignated Alibates Flint Quarries NM 1978)
Aug. 31 Fort Scott Historic Area, Kansas (redesignated Fort Scott NHS and acquisition authorized 1978)
Sept. 1 Delaware Water Gap NRA, Pennsylvania and New Jersey
Sept. 21 Assateague Island NS, Maryland and Virginia
Oct. 22 Roger Williams NMem, Rhode Island
Nov. 11 Amistad NRA, Texas

1966

March 10 Cape Lookout NS, North Carolina
June 20 Fort Union Trading Post NHS, North Dakota and Montana
June 30 Chamizal NMem, Texas
July 23 George Rogers Clark NHP, Indiana
Sept. 9 San Juan Island NHP, Washington
Oct. 15 Guadalupe Mountains NP, Texas
Oct. 15 Pictured Rocks NL, Michigan
Oct. 15 Wolf Trap Farm Park for the Performing Arts, Virginia
Nov. 2 Theodore Roosevelt Inaugural NHS, New York
Nov. 5 Indiana Dunes NL, Indiana

Details of Expansion 21

1967

May 26 John Fitzgerald Kennedy NHS, Massachusetts
Nov. 27 Eisenhower NHS, Pennsylvania

1968

March 12 National Visitor Center, District of Columbia (abolished 1981)
April 5 Saugus Iron Works NHS, Massachusetts
Oct. 2 Appalachian NST, Maine, New Hampshire, Vermont, Massachusetts, Connecticut, New York, New Jersey, Pennsylvania, Maryland, West Virginia, Virginia, North Carolina, Tennessee, and Georgia
Oct. 2 Lake Chelan NRA, Washington
Oct. 2 North Cascades NP, Washington
Oct. 2 Redwood NP, California
Oct. 2 Ross Lake NRA, Washington
Oct. 2 Saint Croix NSR, Minnesota and Wisconsin (assigned to NPS 1969)
Oct. 17 Carl Sandburg Home NHS, North Carolina
Oct. 18 Biscayne NM, Florida (incorporated in Biscayne NP 1980)

1969

Jan. 16 Mar-A-Lago NHS, Florida (abolished 1980)
Jan. 20 Marble Canyon NM, Arizona (incorporated in Grand Canyon NP 1975)
Aug. 20 Florissant Fossil Beds NM, Colorado
Dec. 2 Lyndon B. Johnson NHS, Texas (redesignated a NHP 1980) Dec. 2 William Howard Taft NHS, Ohio

1970

Sept. 26 Apostle Islands NL, Wisconsin Oct. 10 Fort Point NHS, California
Oct. 16 Andersonville NHS, Georgia
Oct. 21 Sleeping Bear Dunes NL, Michigan

1971

Jan. 8 Chesapeake and Ohio Canal NHP, District of Columbia, Maryland, and West Virginia (incorporated Chesapeake and Ohio Canal NM)
Jan. 8 Gulf Islands NS, Florida and Mississippi
Jan. 8 Voyageurs NP, Minnesota

1972

March 1 Buffalo NR, Arkansas

June 16 John F. Kennedy Center for the Performing Arts, District of Columbia (date of NPS acquisition)
Aug. 17 Puukohola Heiau NHS, Hawaii
Aug. 25 Grant-Kohrs Ranch NHS, Montana
Aug. 25 John D. Rockefeller, Jr., Memorial Parkway, Wyoming
Oct. 9 Longfellow NHS, Massachusetts
Oct. 21 Hohokam-Pima NM, Arizona
Oct. 21 Thaddeus Kosciuszko NMem, Pennsylvania
Oct. 23 Cumberland Island NS, Georgia
Oct. 23 Fossil Butte NM, Wyoming
Oct. 25 Lower Saint Croix NSR, Minnesota and Wisconsin
Oct. 27 Gateway NRA, New York and New Jersey
Oct. 27 Golden Gate NRA, California

Part II: The Addition of the "New Alaska Parklands" and Why It Should be Considered Part of the Expansion of "The Hartzog Years"

by Frank P. Sherwood

It took many years for many of the virgin territories of Alaska to be incorporated in the national park system, and it was only in 1980 that much of the mission was finally accomplished, as is described in the text that follows. But the struggle began much earlier, and the foundations were firmly laid in the Hartzog years. Here is what will be found later in this book (in extremely summary form) about the singular role Hartzog played in these events.

> He [Sen. Alan Bible] asked Hartzog to provide him the language needed for inclusion in the bill. The result was a provision that reserved 80 million acres, four million more than Hartzog proposed, largely for parks and wildlife preservation. It appeared that this great expansion in Alaska would occur during the Hartzog tenure. For a variety of reasons, not unusual in the nation's political processes, it did not. It was nearly a decade later that the Alaska National Interest Lands Conservation Act of 1980 was passed. It added more than 43 million acres to the park system and more than 53 million acres to the national wildlife system, a total of 96 million acres. The concept was essentially that which George Hartzog had been developing since assuming the Directorship in 1964. Several of the key figures involved in the 1980 legislation wrote to Hartzog in 1985:
>
>> We equate you with the Redwoods, with the North Cascades, and—though few know this—with being the architect of the Alaska National Interest Land and Conservation Act. Together with Alan Bible and Scoop Jackson you wrote a chapter in the Park Service Book that reduces all other chapters—important as they are—to prologues and epilogues.[2]

The events leading up to the acquisition of the new Alaska parklands in 1980 are therefore included in this description of the Hartzog years.

Part III: "New Alaska Parklands,"
from "Rounding Out the System, 1973–1984"

by Barry Mackintosh [3]

One of the great conservation campaigns of the century produced a fitting climax to this account of the system's evolution: the new national parklands in Alaska. The addition of these enormous acreages to the Park System was one of the far-reaching results of Alaska's admission to the Union in 1959.

The Alaska Native Claims Settlement Act of December 18, 1971, contained a provision of tremendous consequence for the national conservation systems. Section 17(d)(2) of the act directed the Secretary of the Interior "to withdraw from all forms of appropriation under the public land laws ... and from selection under the Alaska Statehood Act, and from selection by Regional Corporations ... up to, but not to exceed, eighty million acres of unreserved public lands in the State of Alaska ... which the Secretary deems are suitable for addition to or creation as units of the National Park, Forest, Wildlife Refuge, and Wild and Scenic Rivers Systems ...." He had two years to make specific recommendations for additions to the four systems from the withdrawn lands, and the recommended lands would remain withdrawn until Congress acted for up to five more years.

On the second anniversary deadline, Secretary Rogers C. B. Morton transmitted his recommendations, which included 32.3 million acres for parklands at a time when the entire system then encompassed some 31 million acres. The recommendations were controversial, especially in Alaska, where there was strong opposition to so much land being removed from potential economic exploitation and other uses incompatible with park status. Bills introduced by both supporters and opponents made little headway until the 95th Congress in 1977–1978, the last two years for legislative action before the withdrawals expired. A strong conservation bill in that Congress introduced by Rep. Morris K. Udall of Arizona, which went beyond the Morton recommendations in significant respects, incorporated the national preserve concept to allow for sport hunting in areas bearing that designation rather than in certain national parks, as Morton had proposed.

A modified version of Udall's H. R. 39 passed the House of Representatives on May 18, 1978, but Senators Mike Gravel and Ted Stevens of Alaska blocked action on a comparable measure in the Senate, and the 95th Congress adjourned in October without an Alaska lands act. The land withdrawals were due to expire on December 18. Faced with this prospect, President Jimmy Carter on December 1 took the extraordinary step of proclaiming 15 new national monuments and two major monument additions on the withdrawn lands. Of the new monuments, two were under Forest Service jurisdiction and two under the Fish and Wildlife Service; the other 11 were additions to the National Park System. (The Fish and Wildlife monuments, Becharof and Yukon Flats, were later incorporated in national wildlife refuges; the Forest Service monuments, Misty Fjords and Admiralty Island, retain their identities under that bureau.)

The national monuments, proclaimed under authority of the 1906 Antiquities Act, were stopgaps; Congress could hardly be expected to provide funds for administering areas it had declined to approve. The purpose was to withhold the areas from other disposition at least until the next Congress could reconsider protective legislation.

Bills were reintroduced in the 96th Congress and a revised H. R. 39 sponsored by Reps. Udall and John Anderson of Illinois passed the House on May 16, 1979. Alaska's senators, allied with a range of commercial interests and sportsmen's groups, again fought to limit additions to the restrictive national park and wildlife refuge systems. A somewhat weaker conservation bill finally cleared the Senate on August 19, 1980. After Ronald Reagan's defeat of President Carter in November, supporters of the House bill decided to accept the Senate bill rather than risk an impasse before Congressional adjournment and a less acceptable bill in years to come. The House approved the Senate measure on November 12, and on December 2 Carter signed into the law the Alaska National Interest Lands Conservation Act (ANILCA).

ANILCA contributed to the National Park System the remarkable total of 47,080,730 acres, exceeding the nearly 45 million acres assigned it by the provisional national monument proclamations and surpassing by nearly 50 percent the 32.3 million acres proposed seven years before. The act converted most of the national monuments to national parks and preserves, the latter permitting sport hunting and trapping. Before December 1978 Alaska had contained one national park, two national monuments, and two national historical parks. After December 1980 its park lands included eight national parks, two national monuments, ten national preserves, two national historical parks, and one wild river.

Mount McKinley National Park was renamed Denali National Park after the Indian name for the mountain and was joined by a Denali National Preserve. Together the park and preserve contain 4,000,000 acres more than the older national park. The old Glacier Bay and Katmai national monuments became national parks, with adjoining national preserves. The Glacier Bay Park and preserve gained some 470,000 acres over the old monument, while the two Katmai areas exceed the old Katmai monument by nearly 1,300,000 acres.

Wrangell-St. Elias National Park contains 8,331,406 acres. Adjacent Wrangell-St. Elias National Preserve contains some 4,873,000 acres. Together they comprise an area larger than the combined area of Vermont and New Hampshire and contain the continent's greatest array of glaciers and peaks above 16,000 feet—among them Mount St. Elias, rising second only to Mount McKinley in the United States. With Canada's adjacent Kluane National Park this is one of the greatest areas of parklands in the world.

Gates of the Arctic National Park, whose 7,498,000 acres lie entirely north of the Arctic Circle, and the 943,000-acre national preserve of the same name include part of the Central Brooks Range, the northernmost extension of the Rockies. Gentle valleys, wild rivers, and numerous lakes complement the jagged mountain peaks.

Adjoining Gates of the Arctic on the west is Noatak National Preserve. Its 6,557,000 acres are drained by the Noatak River, which runs through the 65-mile-long Grand Canyon of the Noatak, and contains a striking array of plant and animal life and hundreds of prehistoric archeological sites in what is the largest untouched river basin in the United States.

Bering Land Bridge National Preserve with 2,774,000 acres on the Seward Peninsula covers a remnant of the land bridge that connected North America and Asia more than 13,000 years ago. Modern Eskimos manage their reindeer herds in and around the preserve, which features rich paleontological and archeological resources, large migratory bird populations, ash explosion craters, and lava flows.

The 2,634,000-acre Lake Clark National Park and the 1,405,500-acre Lake Clark National Preserve are set in the heart of the Chigmit Mountains on the western shore of Cook Inlet, southwest of Anchorage. The 50-mile-long Lake Clark, largest of more than 20 glacial lakes, is fed by hundreds of waterfalls tumbling from the surrounding mountains and its headwaters for an important red salmon spawning ground. Jagged peaks and granite spires have caused the region to be called the Alaskan Alps.

Yukon-Charley Rivers National Preserve protects 115 miles of the Yukon and the entire 88-mile Charley River basin within its 2,517,000 acres. Abandoned cabins and other cultural remnants recall the Yukon's role during the 1898 Alaska gold rush. The Charley, running swift and clear, is renowned for whitewater recreation. Grizzly bears, Dall sheep, and moose are among the abundant wildlife.

Kobuk Valley National Park, another Arctic area of 1,749,000 acres, adjoins the south border of Noatak National Preserve. Its diverse terrain includes the northernmost extent of the boreal forest and the 25-square-mile Great Kobuk Sand Dunes, the largest active dune field in Arctic latitudes. Archeological remains are especially rich, revealing more than 10,000 years of human activity.

Kenai Fjords National Park contains 676,000 acres. On the Gulf of Alaska near Seward, it is named for the scenic glacier-carved fjords along its coast. Above is the Harding Icefield, one of four major ice caps in the United States, from which radiate 34 major glacier arms. Sea lions and other marine mammals abound in the coastal waters.

Cape Krusenstern National Monument, north of Kotzebue on the Chukchi Sea, is the single new Alaskan unit of predominantly cultural rather than natural significance. Containing 656,685 acres, it is by far the largest such area in the system. One hundred fourteen lateral beach ridges formed by changing sea levels and wave action display chronological evidence of 5,000 years of marine mammal hunting by Eskimo peoples. Older archeological sites are found inland.

Of the 1980 Alaska parks, the smallest is Aniakchak National Monument, whose 136,955 acres lie on the harsh Aleutian Peninsula southwest of Katmai. It is adjoined by the 466,238-acre Aniakchak National Preserve. Their central feature is the great Aniakchak Caldera, a 30-square-mile crater of a collapsed volcano. Within the caldera are a cone from later volcanic activity, lava flows, explosion pits, and Surprise Lake, which is heated by hot springs and cascades through a rift in the crater wall.

ANILCA also designated 13 wild rivers for Park Service administration. Twelve are entirely within parks, monuments, and preserves and are not listed as discrete units of the system. Part of the remaining one, Alagnak Wild River, lies outside and westward of Katmai; it is therefore counted separately. It offers salmon sport fishing and whitewater floating.

Overall, the size and quantity of the new Alaska parklands is matched fully by their superlative quality. While political and economic arguments had been raised against them, few if any challenged the inherent scenic, scientific, and cultural merits that made the lands so clearly eligible for the National Park system. The system has been immeasurably enriched by their inclusion.

Notes

1. *The National Parks: Shaping the System* (Washington, DC: Division of Publications, National Park Service, Department of the Interior, 1984), 62–78.
2. See pg. 92, this volume.
3. "Rounding Out the System." *The National Parks: Shaping the System* (Washington, D.C. : Division of Publications,1984), 88–91.

Chapter Three

GEORGE B. HARTZOG, JR.: THE MAN AND THE MISSION[1]

by Frank P. Sherwood

What is important to understand about George B. Hartzog, Jr. is that he had only one career aspiration. That was to be Director of the National Park Service. It was a position he assumed January 8, 1964 and held until December 31, 1972, serving three Secretaries of the Interior and two Presidents. His service totaled nearly nine years.[2]

It is with the discharge of these responsibilities that George B. Hartzog, Jr., achieved uncommon success on any standard of achievement and therefore deserves to be regarded as a *great* Director of the National Park Service. This chapter will be primarily concerned with that movement toward greatness, recognizing that neat cutoff points do not occur in life. It will be concerned not only with his nine years of leadership but also with the remarkable way in which he handled the period after his summary dismissal by President Richard Nixon in 1972.

The analysis of leadership performance is inevitably complicated by the organizational nature of responsibility. Individuals typically have considerable control over their behavior; and accountability for action is fairly direct. Hartzog, in contrast, had 13,000 employees whose energies and resources he had to mobilize and direct toward the broad goal of preserving and utilizing the national parks in the public interest. Further, those 13,000 employees were deployed as guardians of about 30 million acres of land, one per cent of all the land in the nation.[3] While it is clear that Hartzog remained an individual, the appraisal of his nine years of leadership must be framed in organizational terms. It is not entirely a matter of who and what he was as an individual but also what the organization was and what it accomplished.

ASSESSING HARTZOG'S PERFORMANCE

In the context of the National Park Service and its relatively unique responsibilities, it appears that there are two standards against which to evaluate Hartzog's leadership: (a) quantitative indicators of performance; and (b) qualitative appraisals of the Hartzog time from a variety of constituencies, including Congressmen, the media, advocacy groups, and members of the Park Service bureaucracy.

Accomplishments: The Quantitative Side

There are no easy quantitative ways in which to measure the performance of the Park Service in the Hartzog tenure or to contrast his leadership service with his predecessors and his successors. Further, conflict exists over what the Park Service should do in its role as overlord of highly significant national resources. Even so, there does appear to be one area of consensus. It is that the system should be continually expanded, in order that more of the nation's heritage will be preserved and protected, and thus made fully available for the enjoyment of future generations. A consequent test of leadership performance, therefore, is the change in physical scale of the parks in a particular Director's term.

Park Expansion

By this standard Hartzog far outstripped other NPS Directors. It was during his tenure that the greatest parks expansion was recorded. As Bill Connelly wrote in the *Richmond Times Dispatch* at the time of Hartzog's dismissal in 1972, "Even Hartzog's enemies concede, however, that he had a remarkable record of achievement in expanding the park system. During his administration 77 [sic] units totaling 2.7 million acres were added..."[4] The *Washington Evening Star* editorialized:

> The record speaks impressively. Since Hartzog took charge in 1964, national parks acreage has swelled by more than two and one-half million acres and 78 [sic] new parks have been created... At Wolf Trap Farm, the cultural national park concept was initiated...St. Louis has its splendid urban national park beside the Mississippi with the graceful Saarinen Arch towering as the Gateway to the West.[5]

In 1985 the National Park Service published a monograph, *The National Parks: Shaping the System*, tracing the history of national park development from its origins in the Hot Springs Reservation in Arkansas in 1832 to its status 152 years later. It is noteworthy that the period 1964-72 was singled out for special treatment and was further labeled, "The Hartzog Years."[6] The nine years was the shortest period of time covered in the several sections of the book. Justification for this special treatment is revealed in the report that 69 of the 334 NPS units were authorized or acquired during the Hartzog period, nearly three-quarters as many as had been added in the previous 30 years.⁷ Hartzog's role and relationships were described in the following terms:

> The Director during these years was George B. Hartzog Jr., who came to the office at a favorable time. Mission 66, the ten-year program of upgrading the parks, was coming to an end. Stewart L. Udall, Secretary of the Interior, found in Hartzog a willing ally who would push Udall's expansionist and activist park policy for President Lyndon B. Johnson's "Great Society." Backed by a rejuvenated system and the Secretary's support, Hartzog was set to put his imprint on the Service.⁸

Not only did the scale of the parks grow but also their diversity. The Park Service publication identified three main categories into which the additions could be placed:

a. Natural areas: ten new parks; two national monuments upgraded to park status; and five new national monuments.

b. Historical areas: led all others with 35 essentially new arrivals; nine new Presidential sites [a fifth new Lincoln site brought him into a tie with Teddy Roosevelt]; two former Army posts; four homes of important literary figures; and six others, such as the C and O Canal in Washington, D. C.

c. Recreational areas: added at the "remarkable average of three per year" for a total of 27; nearly half were national seashores [of which there were five] and reservoir-related areas; four national lakeshores; four reservoir recreation areas; two scenic rivers; two performing arts centers [Kennedy Center and Wolftrap]; two urban recreation areas, and the John D. Rockefeller Jr. Parkway in Wyoming. It was noted that the authorization of the Ozark National Scenic Riverway, in which Hartzog had a particularly personal part, "…was a forerunner of the comprehensive Wild and Scenic Rivers Act of October 2, 1968, which instituted a national wild and scenic rivers system based on conservationist philosophy."⁹

Some measure of Hartzog's involvement and aggressive leadership in these developments was captured by John McPhee in *The New Yorker*.¹⁰ Describing a typical staff meeting, McPhee quotes Hartzog: "…we've got to move on Alaska. Alaska is hot right now. What is the list of the things we want?" He then answered his own question: "Klondike Gold Rush International Historical Park, Wood-Tikchik National Recreation Area, the Lake Clark Pass, extensions to Mount McKinley National Park, Gates of the Arctic National Park, and St. Elias Range—fifteen million acres in all."[11] William Everhart, whose book on the Park Service is a basic reference, reported that Hartzog's personal involvement in "the most accelerated growth in Park Service history" caused many to refer to his tenure as the "Hartzog era."[12] He commented further:

> The seventh Director, George B. Hartzog, Jr., who served from 1964 through 1972, was among all Directors the closest to Mather [Stephen T. Mather, the Service's much revered first Director, who served from 1914 until his death in 1929] in style. Not at all slavish about following established procedures, he refreshed the outlook of a tradition-loving organization with a constant stream of fresh ideas. Perhaps most important, he knew how to make the ideas work…During his regime sixty-two new parks were established. [It should be noted that Everhart apparently counted only those that were established, not authorized.][13]

Increased Usage

As might be expected, expansion also brought increased patronage. Visitors to the park installations more than doubled in the Hartzog years to 213 million people.[14] Thus, by virtually any quantitative measure, it appeared that Hartzog had led the National Park Service to a peak of acceptance and support.

Fourth Longest Tenure

Finally, George Hartzog had the fourth longest tenure of any NPS Director. While there need not be a correlation between length in office and quality of performance, leaders in highly visible Federal posts, such as Director of the Park Service, can afford to alienate only a part of their constituency. The longest tenure was that of Stephen Mather, the first Director who served from 1915 to 1929, fourteen years; Conrad Wirth (1951–1964) had the second longest, slightly over twelve years; Newton Drury (1940–1951) had the third longest, eleven; and Hartzog's nine-year tenure is fourth. All these Directors served under several Presidents of both political parties and thus underscored the professionalism of the system. Hartzog himself served two Presidents: Johnson, a Democrat; and Nixon, a Republican; and three Secretaries of the Interior, Stewart Udall (in the Johnson term) and Walter Hickel and Rogers C. B. Morton (in the Nixon), were his supervisors. Everhart reports, "Secretary Hickel ousted all of his bureau chiefs except Hartzog, backing off when it became apparent that Hartzog was highly respected in Congress and that if he were fired, the Nixon programs for Interior would receive a cold reception."[15]

In a Federal climate that has become increasingly politicized over the last 40 years, with corresponding declines in the length of service of government executives, Hartzog's duration in office becomes more noteworthy. He is the last Director to have had a substantial tenure. In this sense the raw capacity to survive does become a measure of leadership effectiveness. Thus, these quantitative measures argue that Hartzog was a great Director of the National Park Service.

Qualitative Appraisals of Performance

Perhaps the single greatest evidence of the respect in which Hartzog's performance was held can be seen in Everhart's statement, "The Park Service was never held in higher esteem than in 1972, the 100th anniversary of Yellowstone."[16] He observed that, "…his [Hartzog's] departure came only a few weeks after what may have been the agency's finest hour, when it was host to the second World Conference on the parks."[17] Certainly one cannot imagine a better way to conclude nine years of service. The conference attracted 1,200 delegates from 83 nations, all assembled at Yellowstone to commemorate its founding; and "…Director Hartzog presided over the most estimable meeting of the world park community ever held."[18]

There have been three occasions when there has been an outpouring of appraisals of George Hartzog's performance as Director: (a) when he was fired at the beginning of Nixon's second term in late 1972; (b) when the George B. Hartzog, Jr. Visitors Center at the Jefferson National Expansion Memorial was formally established in 1985; and (c) when his book, *Battling for the National Parks*, was published in 1988. Each occasion provided an opportunity for a variety of individuals to comment on his performance.

AT THE TIME OF HIS DISMISSAL

President Nixon's resolve to sweep out all those who had even remote ties to the past probably meant that Hartzog's days were numbered. Still, it is significant that Hartzog, whose position was a formal appointment of the Secretary of the Interior, was actually fired by the President. Much of that story is reported by Hartzog himself in his book. Interestingly, his own network kept him completely informed in respect to the President's intentions; and one member of that network was former President Johnson who asked the Treasury Secretary John Connally to intercede in support of Hartzog. The word back was that Nixon was intransigent. Indeed, Hartzog learned that Rogers Morton's reappointment as Secretary of the Interior was conditioned on his firing Hartzog. Morton and Hartzog had an extremely close working relationship; and Hartzog's account reveals the occasion was a particularly painful one for Morton.[19]

Why was the President so negative towards Hartzog? The story behind his attitude suggests moral differences between the nation's chief executive and the Director of the National Park Service. The basic facts are detailed by Everhart:

> When the Park Service was acquiring the land for Biscayne National Monument, not far from Nixon's Florida retreat, it purchased the Biscayne Club. This imposing lodge was formerly owned by a group of wealthy sportsmen, of whom Nixon's pal, Bebe Rebozo, was a shareholder. As was customary, the Park Service continued to employ the resident caretaker, who happened to be Rebozo's brother-in-law. Before the Park Service takeover, the caretaker had been granted exclusive use of the club's boat dock; but, after he was placed on the Federal payroll, this privilege ended and the dock was opened to the public. As it turned out, Nixon and Rebozo had been the actual beneficiaries of the private dock, using it as an occasional stop on their jaunts in the Rebozo pleasure boat. Nixon was furious with Hartzog for not taking the necessary steps to maintain the dock as a Presidential enclave. Thenceforth he preferred to anchor out in the bay rather than share the dock with the public.[20]

Hartzog's network had let him know that he had powerful enemies in the Nixon administration. After persistent questioning of his informants, one name that emerged was Rebozo. Horace Albright, the second Director of the Park Service and still a much respected and active participant in its affairs in 1972, asked Hartzog what he could have done to offend Rebozo."Beats me," the Director replied, "I never met the man." Then he recalled the Biscayne National Monument affair. Albright quickly responded, "That's it, and you are in lots of trouble..."[21] Thus did the Park Service Director's ethic of making facilities available to all the people run afoul of a chief executive's insistence that his private interest comes first.

A sampling of editorial opinion suggests that there was both satisfaction with the Hartzog performance and also anxiety over the break with the career neutrality that had characterized the Director's position. The *Washington Evening Star* declared that Hartzog would be "hard to match as an effective and innovative administrator" and labeled his dismissal "lamentable and surprising."[22] Juxtaposed with the positive appraisal of Hartzog was strong opposition to politicizing the appointment. The *St. Louis Post-Dispatch* declared that President Nixon had "cast a cloud of doubt over any spirit of rededication to the park system by putting at the head of the National Park Service the first political appointee of its history."[23]

AT THE TIME OF THE DEDICATION OF THE HARTZOG VISITORS CENTER

In 1985, the dedication of the George B. Hartzog, Jr. Visitors Center at the Jefferson Expansion National Memorial was the occasion for a major recognition of Hartzog's accomplishments. Many of the appraisals came from people within the Park Service, from Congressmen, and from others with deep involvements in the national parks.

Donald Hodel, then the Secretary of the Interior, wrote:

...Your record is a record shared by great leaders in any field; it is a record of a man whose vision allowed him to maximize the accomplishments that opportunity afforded...The lasting effects of your career are clear in the physical legacy you have left. Perhaps more important is an intangible legacy; you left behind an organization that remains infused with your spirit and drive for achievement.[24]

Roy Taylor, a retired congressman who had been deeply involved with Hartzog as Chairman of the National Parks Sub-Committee of the House, described him as a "doer, an activist...His work has made progress a key word." He said he could always count on him for "sound leadership and advice."[25] The President of the Wilderness Society declared that Hartzog had brought "great vision and bold leadership" to the Service. He continued, "Your determination and accomplishments in expanding the national park system are a hallmark which will be long remembered and deeply appreciated by many future generations."[26]

Letters to Hartzog from current and retired employees were similarly laudatory. Many referred to his positive characteristics: he was honest, knowledgeable, and hard-working; and he had personal ingenuity, an ability to retain facts, and managerial astuteness. Others were comparative in their statements, one pronouncing him the "greatest in all aspects" and another declaring that his "mastery of the job has not been equaled." An official who had worked 25 years in the private sector before joining NPS said that he had "rubbed elbows with some very capable executives," but "none were your equal."

In still other cases there was reference to specific instances and personal benefits associated with him. One remembered a personal call when he was seriously ill in the hospital, declaring it gave him a "big lift." A second talked of the Hartzog years as "exciting" and "a golden age for the Service and for us as individuals." A third pronounced it a "rare privilege" to work for him and said he still cherished "the opportunity you gave us to grow and flourish under your direction."[27]

While it must be recognized that these letters were part of a conscious effort to honor him for his contributions, it is impressive that they came 13 years after his leadership responsibilities had ended. There could be little doubt that he was much valued by the letter writers.

At the Time of the Publication of His Book in 1988

The introduction to Hartzog's book published in 1988 was written by his boss for five years, former Secretary of the Interior Stewart Udall.[28] Udall's high regard and respect for his former Park Service Director was clearly evident. In many respects the most eloquent appraisal of the Hartzog performance came from Wallace Stegner, well-known author, professor, environmental activist, and former Chairman of the Secretary of the Interior's Advisory Board on National Parks. He described Hartzog as the "toughest, savviest, and most effective bureau chief who ever operated in that political alligator hole"; and he went on, "Among distinguished public administrators he was one of the most distinguished, one of the friendliest, and one of the most honest." Finally, he declared, "The National Park Service has never since been the model high-morale Federal bureau that it was during George Hartzog's tenure."[29]

Institutionally, the Hartzog era was a high point for the organization; and, logically, the Director must be assumed to have contributed substantially to such organizational quality. Further, the many personal evaluations of Hartzog from a wide diversity of sources inside and outside the Park Service are highly positive. The label, "Hartzog Years," seems to epitomize the scale and consequence of his leadership contributions.

Occupying the Role: Dynamics of Appointment as Director, Interview with Conrad Wirth

Some perspective on this man can be obtained from a description of the circumstances of his appointment as Director. The appointment did not automatically come to George Hartzog. The National Park Service had attracted many able people over the years; and it was essentially a closed career system. One started at the bottom and worked up. A promotion for one person meant movement all along the hierarchical line for others. Comparatively speaking, Hartzog was a relative newcomer when he had conversations about his future with Director Conrad Wirth in 1962. Hartzog had entered the Service in 1946 and thus had a seniority of 16 years, low in the Park Service hierarchy; still, Wirth noted that his performance as Director of the Jefferson National Expansion Memorial in St. Louis [involving the construction of the Gateway Arch] had been "excellent."[30] With an offer in hand to become executive director of Downtown St. Louis, Inc. at a much greater salary, Hartzog told Wirth that he preferred to stay in the Park Service but felt ready for a new assignment. Hartzog writes that the response was, "…that there were no major superintendent vacancies, that I had no regional office experience, and that I would have to get in line. However, the Associate Director's job was vacant and had been for months. I suggested that if he filled it, there would be a vacancy—never dreaming that he would appoint me as Associate Director. He would make no commitment to fill the job."[31]

Outstanding Performance in St. Louis

Hartzog had "fallen in love" with the Park Service. The higher salary offered in St. Louis obviously made little difference to him; but a challenging assignment and an opportunity for even greater responsibilities in the future did. Clearly, he was offered the position with Downtown St. Louis because of his great success in the Gateway Arch project, an accomplishment that also did not go unnoticed in the Park Service. The Arch, located at the Jefferson National Expansion Memorial in St. Louis, was designed by Saarinen and is one of the great architectural sites in the world.[32] In his *New Yorker* profile McPhee quotes Udall, "…Had it not been for Hartzog there would be no Arch. It was Hartzog who took a set of plans that had been lying dormant for fifteen years and built the great Arch of St. Louis."[33] The way in which Hartzog's accomplishments were viewed at the higher levels of the Department of Interior is to be found in Udall's further comments:

> In 1960 Congress said no to the Arch. Any other Park Service ranger would have said, 'O. K., Where am I to be sent now? Back to the Great Smokies? Out to Alaska to count blankets?' But not George. He kept at it until funds were appropriated.
>
> George was a lawyer. That is why they had him in St. Louis. They had never built anything bigger than an outhouse before.
>
> When the Arch was halfway up, the contractor was losing money, so he stopped work, saying the structure was unsafe. Two legs, three hundred feet high, were sticking out of the ground. Hartzog said to the contractor, "Listen, I ordered an Arch and I want an Arch."[34]

Monumental as it was, the Arch alone did not occupy Hartzog's full time. For a number of months he was spending all his weekends, plus one or two nights during the week, at meetings and site inspections in the Ozark Rivers area about 150 miles distant from St. Louis. When Hartzog had assumed the St. Louis position in 1960, Howard Baker, then the deputy NPS Director, asked him to work on another project that seemed to be going nowhere, the Ozark Rivers National Monument. The idea was to bring these rivers, notably the Current and Jack's Fork, into the national parks system. Opposition came from many sources; indeed, Hartzog did not go back to St. Louis one night because sand had been poured in the gas tank of his car.

Secretary Udall was enthused about the rivers project and made a two-day trip to the Current River in 1961 to promote the proposal. He described the encounter with Hartzog to reporter McPhee in these terms:

> I met him on the Current River, in Missouri, in 1962. We were trying to make the Current a national river, and a group of us made a two-day float trip there. George…and I rode in the same boat, and I felt that in those two days I really got to know him well…This was group of outdoor people, who were in their element. The Current was going to be the first national river. We hadn't done anything like it before. George knew all the arguments, all the facts, although the Current River is a hundred and fifty miles from St. Louis and the project was not part of his job.[35]

Thus Hartzog was establishing his credentials with the Secretary at a time when changes were brewing in the executive suite of the National Park Service. Wirth writes that he had by that time begun to contemplate retirement; and he leaves the impression that there were stresses in his relations with the upper echelons of the Department of Interior.[36] At the personal level, for example, it would be hard to envisage the scene of camaraderie with Wirth that Secretary Udall described with Hartzog on the Current River. Further, there appeared to be policy differences. Wirth, a landscape architect, had directed his energy to Mission 66, which was an effort to improve the physical structures of the park. Aside from the fact that Mission 66 was thought by some to have led to over-development, it did not fit particularly well within the priorities of Secretary Udall.[37] Everhart notes that the Kennedy years witnessed the emergence of conservation as a front page item, with concerns for the total environment. And Udall "became the acknowledged Federal spokesman on environmental matters."[38]

There was also conflict within the departmental system. In the last three decades assistant secretaries had assumed policy positions between bureau chiefs and departmental secretaries. These relationships had seldom gone smoothly. Apparently, however, that between Wirth and Assistant Secretary John Carver was particularly bad. Wirth devotes a number of pages in his book to explaining his side of an argument in which Carver accused the Park Service of being unresponsive, unchanging, rooted in its tradition, and unable to cope with shifting priorities.[39] It is inevitable that much of this conflict came to Udall's attention and heightened the need for a change in NPS leadership.

In January, 1963, Director Wirth had lunch with the Secretary and announced his intention to resign in January of the following year. He also secured an agreement that his successor would come from within the ranks of the Service. Subsequently, he provided the Secretary with a list of five recommended persons. One of them was Hartzog, even though he had resigned several months earlier.[40]

The St. Louis Meeting with Secretary Udall: Triggering Event

Earlier, however, Hartzog had had another meeting with Secretary Udall that really cinched his appointment. It occurred in August, 1962, and it again revealed the way in which his accomplishments opened up opportunities for him. It came about because of his "warm, personal friendship" with St. Louis Mayor Raymond Tucker, whom he has described as his "guide and counsel" on the Gateway project.[41] When Secretary Udall was coming to town, the Mayor asked Hartzog to go to the airport for a welcoming. Hartzog describes the sequence of events in these terms:

> We met the Secretary, had a pleasant visit on the way in town during which Mayor Tucker told the Secretary that I had left the NPS and was now working with Downtown St. Louis, Inc. The Secretary expressed surprise. When we arrived at the Jefferson Hotel, the Mayor preceded the Secretary and me through the door. Instead of following, Stewart hung back and asked me why I left. I said, 'Well, I had no future.'
>
> He replied, 'Would being Director be enough future?'
>
> I said, 'Mr. Secretary, it sure would.' He followed the Mayor through the door with me behind him. The subject was not mentioned again during the visit.[42]

Secretary Udall gave himself a greater role in arranging the encounter with Hartzog, according to his interview with McPhee. He declared, "...I heard he had quit the Park Service, because he thought he had no future in it. I went to St. Louis and looked him up and asked him if he would come back and he thought being Director was enough of a future. He said, 'Mr. Secretary, I surely do.'"⁴³

Negotiating the Appointment

Three months after the August encounter, Hartzog again met with Udall, this time in Washington. The Secretary reiterated his intention to make Hartzog the Director. Hartzog recalls an initial shock and his question, "Is Connie Wirth retiring?" The rejoinder was, "He's going to." Hartzog then declared, "Mr. Secretary, I want that job more than anything in the world, but I do not want to be a party to pushing Connie Wirth out."⁴⁴ He said that he would not accept unless Wirth personally invited him to become the Associate Director, with the understanding that the Directorship would come to him on Wirth's retirement. A general agreement was reached, largely with Assistant Secretary Carver, that the process could go forward only with Wirth's full acquiescence. It was Carver who said, "…you are exactly right not to be a party to pushing out Connie Wirth. If you did that, you would bring with you your own enemies and all of Connie Wirth's friends who would become your enemies."⁴⁵ But Hartzog's feeling ran deeper than simple concerns about propriety and politics. He was incensed that a person with Wirth's commitments and record of success had been so cavalierly treated. It was bad for the individual involved; more importantly, it was very bad for the organization and its capacity to get and retain the best people. Thus the condition that Wirth had personally to invite him back as Associate Director.

Shortly after the meeting with Udall and Carver, Hartzog did meet with Wirth and reported that the Associate Director's job had been discussed. Nothing was said about the Directorship. Two months later, Wirth called and made the formal offer of the Associate position; and Hartzog reported in February, 1963.⁴⁶ There is some discrepancy in the accounts of Hartzog and Wirth. Hartzog thought the list of five recommended names was for the Associate Directorship⁴⁷; Wirth is quite clear that they were nominations for his successor. Wirth does not report on the meeting with Hartzog and implies that his succession was his sole preoccupation.⁴⁸ Things proceeded as planned, and the new Director took office in January, 1964.⁴⁹

Insights on Hartzog from the Appointment Experience

The story of Hartzog's appointment provides insight on his personal style and character. The Gateway Arch and Ozark Rivers experiences reveal a person with high achievement motivation, very fortunately directed toward the public interest. Clearly involved is a value of service; but it is profoundly buttressed by the belief in work, hard work as a critical element in dealing with the human circumstance. Hartzog's was a proud family, impoverished by the Depression. That situation called for even greater effort, in which his mother played a major role. Hartzog recalls, "She worked hard. She pulled the family through. She believed you couldn't fail to achieve anything if you just worked. She encouraged me and instilled in me the responsibility for working."[50]

Hartzog brought great psychic and physical energy to his work ethic. The virtually concurrent tasks of building the Gateway Arch and putting together the nation's first scenic river demanded far more than most people are able or willing to give. Hartzog fully met Harlan Cleveland's requirement that an executive must possess "animal energy."[51]

It is noteworthy that Hartzog was given two stalled assignments. Congress had appropriated no money for the Arch, and the Ozark Rivers project at the time was just a dream. Howard Baker, the deputy Director, wrote, "Connie and I really had a great stroke of luck when we decided to move George into the St. Louis spot. He had all the various talents that we needed to get the job done."[52] Baker, in particular, gave Hartzog the Ozarks chore and must have trusted to more than luck in making the assignment. He may well have seen in Hartzog an "unwarranted optimism," to use Cleveland's phrase. Goals are to be met, and there can be no excuse for failure to do so. Thus, what seemed to be insurmountable obstacles for most were simply problems to Hartzog.

Further, Hartzog brought to his tasks a profound understanding that the exercise of leadership is a collaborative undertaking. That is a particular truth for the public executive. As will be discussed in greater detail at a later point in this chapter, Hartzog possessed a deep belief in the democratic process. In many respects the supreme satisfaction is to play a key role in bringing about a desired collective action. It requires the most of a person; and success thus brings the satisfaction of having been challenged and having used one's resources fully. Unlike many professionals, including his colleagues in the Park Service, Hartzog savored the give-and-take of the political process. In the case of the Gateway Arch, his accomplishments were of two kinds: (a) persuading the Congress to provide necessary funds; and (b) using those resources skillfully to build a national treasure. In the case of the Ozark Rivers project, the accomplishment was engineering consent for the creation of the nation's first scenic waterway. It is in the engagement of disparate and conflicting political forces that Hartzog seems to have been at his best.

It is clear that Hartzog had his own internal navigation system. While he was frank to profess his love of the National Park Service and his desire to stay on its rolls, he saw the relationship as a reciprocal one. In return for his loyalty and service, the NPS was expected to provide him opportunities to use his talents fully, to confront important challenges, and to grow as an individual. What disturbed him greatly was that the essence of the bargain was broken by Conrad Wirth. Again, it was an organizational indictment, not a personal injury. True to his own ideals, he left the Park Service. It is sad to contemplate how close the meetings with Wirth came to ending Hartzog's contributions to the Service; and, indeed, it is reassuring that Secretary Udall insisted on bringing this scarce human resource back to the service of the nation. The intervention by the Secretary was desperately needed. There was really no way that Hartzog could have compromised his belief in the reciprocal obligations of employer and employee. Conrad Wirth simply had not held up his end of the bargain as NPS leader.

The Director's Job

George B. Hartzog, Jr. assumed the Director's position the year of the Watts Riots (1964). The racial strife in Los Angeles presaged the beginning of nearly a decade of national ferment, an ill-fated Viet Nam war, generational conflict, and a belated discovery of the severity of the nation's urban problems. For most people it would not be regarded as the best of times to occupy a position of national leadership. Hartzog thought differently. It was a time of opportunity to fix a lot of things that seemed irreparable.

The Director in the Middle of Profound Policy Conflict

The nature of public leadership in a democracy makes it difficult, however, for even the strongest and most committed individual to move unswervingly toward a desired goal. Further, the navigation of Park policy must occur within a context of profound, long-standing differences on how the parks should be conceived and managed. At the one extreme are the disciples of John Muir who view the parks and everything in them as God-given. Every living creature is in the parks by design and deserves protection; and humankind has no right to assert its priorities over the other elements of the eco-system. The obligation, then, is to preserve these sites exactly as they are. At the other extreme are the demands for transportation, amenities, and accommodations that will permit multitudes of people to enjoy these natural wonders, which of course become less natural with such intrusions. The concessionaires who insist on the right to fly sightseeing airplanes over the Grand Canyon are perhaps at the extreme of these use claims.

Such disputes did not originate with Hartzog but were likely exacerbated by his dogged determination to discover the public interest in what Stegner termed "a political alligatorhole." McPhee reported that Congressmen were upset in 1969 when there were rumors of Hartzog's impending departure. He wrote,

> They admire his effort to give new directions to the park system... They are sympathetic to some of Hartzog's problems within the Administration. "Sometimes he gets clobbered by the Secretary or the White House," [U. S. Representative John P.] Saylor has said. "Sometimes he comes in here in a straitjacket. He is not always free to act as an individual. He is told policy. It takes a strong, strong man to overcome the political shenanigans that go on here in Washington. His is supposed to be a nonpolitical job, but it's not."[53]

Hartzog's Policy Position

Hartzog was well aware of the conflicts within which his position placed him. Connelly reported that Hartzog saw himself as seeking a balance between those who wanted parks to provide more roads and conveniences and those who wanted to protect the natural areas from being overrun by people."That's the story of my life," Connelly quoted him, "I'm caught between the extremists...and you'll never please either side [the conservationists or the recreationists] if you truly protect the public interest in the parks."[54]

The first chapter of Hartzog's book is entitled, "Whose Parks Are These?" and the essential point of the question is the conflict between preservationist and park user. While parklands at the beginning of the park system in 1872 were to be preserved from injury or spoliation, the construction of roads and bridle paths was authorized. Over the years the conflict between preservation and usage has reappeared and was reinforced: in 1906 with extended powers to build roads and to make leases with concessionaires; in 1916 in the establishment of a Park Service with freedom to establish accommodations in the parks; and in 1965 in the Concessions Policy Act where, "in glorious ambiguity, it [the Congress] reaffirmed both preservation and use…"[55] Hartzog continues,

> In the United States the people are sovereign. America's national parks are the special creations of the people through their elected representatives in Congress…The purpose of the national parks remains in hot dispute. Is it their purpose to be host to exuberant youth on a frolic or privately-owned camping spaces for congenial club members? Protectors of gene pools to sustain life or parking sites for relaxing in recreational motor vehicles bringing all the modern conveniences from the home left behind? Preserves for scientists to search for knowledge and understanding of the web of life or a sanctuary for the poor and the underprivileged among us to protest against the ravages of poverty and the indignity of justice too long denied.[56]

Harzog's own comments make it quite clear that he rejected extremes of both preservation and use. The very idea of the park suggested human involvement in his mind. He was quoted as saying, "A park by definition is an area that is set aside for the use and benefit of the people. Therefore, there has got to be appropriate use designed into a park or, by definition, it is not a park."[57] It also must be borne in mind that Hartzog was living through a highly turbulent period of American life when public officials were desperately seeking ways of reducing extreme social tensions. The experiencing of nature, Hartzog believed, was an uplifting, essentially spiritual, event in which all Americans should share. Such benefits for the individual would also bring societal gains through a greater sense of partnership and participation in the system as a whole.

McPhee reports that Hartzog had two principal goals: (a) to maintain the park system's vast existing apparatus and (b) to give it a new emphasis toward the cities. He quotes a Hartzog subordinate, "We used to be trying to catch up to development in established parks, but George is trying to find the needs of the seventies. Those who identify the natural scene as the true purview of the Park Service think of him as a renegade."[58]

Within this context an incident reported by McPhee suggests how Hartzog aroused the ire of the preservationists. The occasion involved the planning for the use of prime Washington D. C. land where World War I "temporary" buildings had stood for more than 50 years. With the removal of the buildings, the Park Service was to receive custody of the land. The question was how it was to be used. One of Hartzog's assistant Directors had been reported as saying that lawns would fill the space. McPhee picks up the story:

> "The hell they will," Hartzog says."Nat Owings wants to put rose gardens and a restaurant there. The last thing we need in downtown Washington is more grass. We've got grass coming out of our ears in this city, and in summer we let it turn brown. We're up to our noses in horticulturists who don't know enough not to water grass when it gets hot. We need more vistas like a Buick needs a fifth hole. I don't think this is Paris. The strength and heart of Washington is to reflect this country, which is virile and informal and friendly."[59]

Opposition Emerges

As might be expected, such positions did not receive the approbation of the conservationists. Over time, opposition to Hartzog mounted, both inside and outside the Park Service. That from inside was fairly muted. The outside voices were clearly more strident. By the time of his removal in 1972, the press was acknowledging such antagonists, though specifics were sparse. Two people identified as seeking his dismissal were George Alderson, head of legislative affairs at Friends of the Earth, and Michael Frome, a writer. The basic charge was that he had come down on the side of development. Alderson and Secretary of the Interior Rogers Morton exchanged letters, which appeared in the journal, *Parks and Recreation*.

Six of nine charges made by Alderson involved development questions: Hartzog was "using every trick" to sabotage the Wilderness Act; he wanted to intrude on the wilderness with two tramways; in the case of Mammoth Caves he wanted no wilderness protection at all; the Director wanted to open "motor nature trails" in wild areas; he allowed concessionaires to keep their business secret from the public; and he made "political deals involving the giveaway of lands." The other three charges were of a management nature and involved turning the parks over to "mere administrators;" too rapid transfers of superintendents and ranger personnel; and the use of transfers as a reprisal mechanism.[60] Secretary Morton responded in the strongest possible terms, declaring his rejection of all the accusations. He wrote, "The National Park System has experienced a great period of expansion under Director Hartzog's determined leadership. Throughout this period the goals of the National Park Service have been met…Your unsupported allegation that Mr. Hartzog is intentionally destroying the national parks is totally and absolutely rejected…"[61]

There was considerable editorial comment on these issues at the time of Hartzog's resignation, of which an editorial in the *Washington Post* appears typical. While it noted a need for change and reform, it gave Hartzog many plaudits:

> The eight years of his reign over the national parks agency have been an extremely challenging, transitional time, during which the country's great parks have been subjected to unprecedented stress, in some cases amounting to a real threat of destruction, from overuse and over-development. Mr. Hartzog, with his keen sense of public and congressional attitudes, has made some progress in shaping new kinds of recreational areas to relieve the pressures on fragile, irreplaceable resources. He has also recorded gains in curbing the use of private vehicles in the most heavily polluted parks.[62]

The view in the press was that the conservationist charges had provided an "extra excuse" for the Nixon group to take an action on which it had already decided. If it had not been for the Nixon attitude, it seems apparent that Hartzog's opposition would have had little impact on Secretary Morton and the Director's many supporters in Congress.

Hartzog himself was almost truculent in defending his record. In his nine years he declared that he had closed about 300 miles of roads within 12 national parks and monuments."The National Parks system has been the greatest preserver of wilderness in the nation, and I will match my record of eliminating developments in parks that were contrary to the preservation of wilderness with that of any other Director in history."[63]

Belief in Democratic Process Central to Hartzog Leadership

The recounting of the fundamental policy issue with which the NPS Director was faced emphasizes the need for a personal compass in negotiating among the claimants to public resources, present and future. One must have a clear sense of role; and, at the level at which Hartzog operated, there was need for a perspective that accepted conflict, ambiguity, and contingency as inherent in such responsibilities. He thought of his job as similar to that of the university President, in that both "…require the skill to herd wild hogs on ice."[64] Such a skill, he remarks, "may be the key qualification for being Director," rather than any particular professional discipline.[65]

McPhee reports the contents of two signs in the Hartzog offices. One, a framed admonition from George Washington, reads: "Do not suffer your good nature, when application is made to say 'Yes' when you should say 'No.'"[66] Another, by the door, says: "Great Spirit, grant that I may not criticize my neighbor until I have walked a mile in his moccasins."[67] What these signs suggest is that the leader should take strong policy positions; but commitments and convictions of others deserve equal recognition. Thus, it was possible for Hartzog to be a very strong leader, as Rep. Saylor observed, and at the same time to accept the importance and legitimacy of differing views. It is important to note that Hartzog did not cower in the wings when a battle clearly was to ensue. He had courage. He let people know where he stood.

It was Hartzog's belief in the democratic process that enabled him to accept and cherish the uncertainties and ambiguities of his leadership experience. In emphasizing that the people were sovereign, Hartzog portrayed himself in full measure as a pluralist. He truly believed that the public interest could be discovered in the active contest of interests and wills. In consequence he did not have to grieve when a battle was lost. If the fight were fair, he could assume the public interest was served. If it were not, the issue was to create a process in which battle could be engaged equitably and openly by all sides. Hartzog had a philosophy about his job that kept him personally fresh and invigorated; at the same time it cannot be imagined how it could have better served the interests of a democratic society.

Personal Qualities/Style

Much of the analysis thus far has been occupied with dimensions of the organization in which Hartzog performed as a leadership example. It should be apparent, however, that he was a special type of individual. Others before and since filled the same organizational slot, but the behavioral outcomes were quite different. To understand Hartzog as a leader it is necessary to think of him as a person oriented by a set of values, energized by varied motivational forces, and endowed with certain dispositions, skills and capacities. At this point it is the human dimension that facilitates an understanding of how it was that Hartzog made his continuing contribution to society.

Leadership Traits

While Hartzog had his detractors, he is generally characterized in positive terms. He has been depicted as bright, forthright, courageous, honest, and committed. Further, such descriptions as "lovable" and "personable" suggest a high personal attractiveness. Rep. Wayne Aspinall labeled him a "fine companion," and former Secretary Udall called him a "happy warrior who exuded reasonableness and good will." Udall added: "His signature was the greeting he invariably extended to ordinary citizens and senators alike: 'Hello, my friend, what can I do for you?'"[68]

Perceptions of Behavior

His intelligence and commitment, along with his zest for work, left little room for indulging inadequacies. Thus the "happy warrior" was not always the visage his subordinates in the Service observed. One view was that he was aloof and imperious; a more contradictory one was that he was gruff but at the same time genial. Within the organization he was described as "...very hard on his people. He cracks the whip. And he has a short fuse." He was also seen as "...too august, too removed a figure."[69] These views were undoubtedly part of a broader perception of Hartzog as a strong, bold, and courageous figure who inspired the contradictory feelings of respect and fear. Hartzog was, in effect, the dominant force in the National Park Service. It was almost inevitable that such a towering presence would excite both positive and negative feelings.

At the same time, within the context of the Hartzog dominance, there was encouragement of open communication and a concern for fair play. Further, it was pointed out that he "...never asks the next guy to do what he wouldn't do himself. He's demanding but his example is high."[70] It is not surprising that Hartzog was regarded as the symbol of an organization, which, as previously reported, had achieved a peak of pride, discipline, and professionalism.

COUPLING OF VISION AND KNOWLEDGE

Bennis and Nanus in their classic work, *Leaders: The Strategies for Taking Charge*, declare that, "All the leaders to whom we spoke seemed to have been masters at selecting, synthesizing, and articulating an appropriate vision of the future."[71] Not only does McPhee's profile in *The New Yorker* reveal Hartzog as a person of great vision, he experienced his mission as compelling. He conceived of himself as an evangelist for the cause of the parks. No personal expenditure was too great or personal contact too small when present or future parks were involved. As McPhee reported:

> He knows that in Washington the shortest distance between two points often includes a trip to Kansas. So he goes. He fears flying, but he goes. He speaks. He drinks. He grins. No guffaws...He travels, too, as an evangelist for his causes...."These things go slow," he says, "You don't make any converts at a big meeting. You have to get one man talking to one man."[72]

Hartzog's sense of direction, industry and commitment allowed him to couple vision and knowledge. It was reported, "George knows the bureau. He knows what's happening here in Interior, he knows what's happening in Morro Castle [California], and he knows what's happening at Mount

The Man and the Mission 51

McKinley [Alaska]."[73] Further, Hartzog never seemed overwhelmed by bureaucratic protocol or detail. He kept his eye on the main ball. One associate declared, "Instead of being preoccupied with the process, he is preoccupied with the idea. I've never heard him discuss reasons why things can't be done."[74] It is not surprising, therefore, that Hartzog was generally regarded as decisive and able to deal with the full complexity and diversity of issues faced by NPS.

Commitment to Parks and Not to Self

Hartzog also likely gained credibility, both inside and outside the Service, because his total commitment was to the parks. No one apparently saw his actions as driven by personal ambition. Indeed, on at least one occasion, he refused a promotion to Assistant Secretary.[75] Apparently, the presence of such selflessness was regarded as refreshingly unique. The Department of Interior was characterized as "…loaded—it's stuffed—with people who are over-ridden by personal ambition. But that is not true of George."[76]

However, Rep. Wayne Aspinall believed there were some risks in Hartzog's compulsive, incessant drive to accomplish his ambitious objectives. While he was obviously very fond of the NPS Director, the Congressman felt that the Director sometimes moved too fast for his own good and skipped over details. He described him as a builder who did not consider the cost of the building. The saving aspect, however, was that Hartzog was able to listen, as Bennis and Nanus say all good leaders must." I say to him, 'No, George. Back up and start over,'" Aspinall reported."He had the personality to be able to back up."[77]

Success in Representing the Parks in the External World: Dealing with Congress

Many of the attributes described above made him a particularly effective representative of Park Service interests in its external environment. Nowhere was that more evident than in his relations with Congress. Had it not been for support from the Hill, the general view is that Hartzog would not have survived the first Nixon administration. While Hartzog's own skills and capacities accounted for much of his success in Congressional relationships, his belief in democratic government and particularly in the

U. S. system positioned him to go to unusual lengths to make it work. Most certainly, his system of values never allowed him to depreciate the importance of the Congress. He reported that when he assumed the Directorship, he personally knew nine Congressmen. When he left the position nine years later, the count was 300. Further, he made clear his commitment to helping them do their jobs. It was reported that, "He will travel…to the remotest corner of any state in the Union to please a senator or a significant congressman."[78]

His performance in the role also did much to gain him support. The Congressmen interviewed by Reporter McPhee evaluated him as the most industrious Director the Service had ever had; admired his effort to give new directions to the system; and felt that he had drawn into the Service people of very high calibre who would not otherwise be there.[79]

The Hartzog style also was an asset. In his frequent testimony before Congressional committees, he was said to speak strongly and colloquially; was well prepared; made his points clearly; and gave the impression he knew what he was talking about, "…which put him in something of a minority among bureaucrats."[80]

In his book, Hartzog provides many case examples of the specific ways in which he worked with Congressional leaders. It was obvious that Hartzog relished the fray; and there could be no gainsaying the fact of battle. As Congress has become increasingly urban in its orientation, support for the parks is not by any means automatic. Hartzog had to use his every wile to cajole, induce, and pressure congressmen to support his programs. As Rep. Saylor said, "He's willing to stand up and fight—he has a healthy respect for Congress, not a callous disregard, but he's willing to stand up and fight. Some days I wouldn't trade him for anyone in the world, and some days I could kill him."[81]

Inside the Bureacracy

While he devoted great energies to his external relations, Hartzog had no doubt that the performance of the system rested with its 13,000 employees. He recognized the importance of communicating system goals, of supporting employees to use themselves as fully as possible in the achievement of those goals, and to make sure that the necessary resources were available to facilitate such work.

THE MAN AND THE MISSION 53

THREE OBJECTIVES

It was, of course, a system in which Hartzog himself had matured; and he had his own feelings about it. It is perhaps fair to say that he had three objectives: (a) to build more of a team environment, in which the psychological distance between the leader and the operating staff was greatly reduced; (b) to develop an institution more attuned to goals and aspirations and less to bureaucratic rules and procedures; and (c) to create a more humanistic system to which highly talented people would be attracted and have the freedom to use their full potential.

In any institution, such aspirations would be difficult to achieve. In an organization highly satisfied with its performance over 50 years, with a deep sense of tradition, and with discrepant views about how a natural area ought to be used, it was a particularly tough task. Nine years turned out to be a short time in which to engineer such changes. Irrespective of the management strategy, the politics within the Service must also be recognized. What happens in its far-flung network of facilities has political, economic, and social significance to communities and interests throughout the nation. Field people inevitably form their own political constituencies.

POLITICS IN PERSONNEL

Illustrative of the political currents continually flowing through the organization is Hartzog's report of dealing with a park superintendent who had long been in his position and made his own political friendships, one of whom was the Secretary of the Interior. Even the Congressman in the district was wary of this superintendent, fearful that he would retire and run against him. The man had become, in Hartzog's terms, a "winger," a lone operator." The result," said Hartzog, "was great difficulty in getting him to do what you thought needed to be done. I resolved I could not have that. I had to be in charge because we had a lot of things going in the state at that time."[82]

First he went to the Secretary to tell him what he was planning. The Secretary asked, "Do you have to?" When Hartzog said yes, the Secretary responded, "Will you be kind about it?" Hartzog then telephoned the superintendent and said he would like to take him and his wife to dinner at a major hotel the end of the week. The social event was held and was pleasant. As they got up to leave the table, Hartzog indicated he would like to have breakfast the next morning."Anything special?" the superintendent asked."Yeah. I would like to know where you would like to go." Things were left at that point until the following day. Hartzog tells the rest of the story in this way:

> The next morning we met for breakfast. I started outlining what I perceived the problems to be. He said, "You don't have to tell me about them. I know them all. If you will let me stay here, I will guarantee you that you will never have another problem with me as long as we live." I said, "If that is the way you feel about it, I can't imagine a person who could do a better job." He went back and became one of the most superb, supportive people in the world.[83]

Candor in Tough Personnel Matters

The experience reported above not only explains the institutional environment within which Hartzog operated but also suggested the open, confronting manner in which he sought to deal with people. His own aspirations were to treat employees as individuals with needs and ambitions. Leaders, he felt, must spend the necessary time to insure that people feel their individuality, are provided full information, and are provided positive ways by which to benefit from the experience. Even with these people-oriented attitudes, Hartzog was not the complete humanist. In his view the needs of the organization were paramount; and Hartzog, as leader, was in the best position to define those requirements. Further, his own values tended to overlay his interpretation of Park Service needs. In the case reported above, the superintendent's continuation in his job really depended on acceptance of the Director's specification of the problems that prompted the confrontation.

The Park Service Type

McPhee reports on what appeared to be a common feeling in the organization, namely that there was a preferred "Park Service type." His example was Lawrence Hadley, then the superintendent of Yosemite National Park [and later a Park Service Director]. He was described as a

> ...young and strong-appearing man with dark features, dark hair, and a suggestion of melancholy in his face. He wears a silver watch-

band with a turquoise inlay and a large silver-and-turquoise shell-inlay ring. He speaks softly and with an unpretentious air of absolute competence. He is Hartzog's idea of the Park Service personified—a man who does anything well and is ready to serve anywhere any time. Hartzog is confident that when Hadley and his wife are asked abruptly to change their personal plans and go to an airport to meet an official visitor, they will do so without pause or regret.[84]

It is probable that none of his 13,000 employees saw Director Hartzog as a capricious leader, typically doling out the goodies to his court jesters. But the demand for an almost superhuman person, endowed with Hartzog-like virtues, created its own image of favoritism. He was accused of reacting emotionally to people, tending to extremes in his feelings about them. McPhee quoted one individual, "He snoops around the parks, and if everything is O. K., the superintendent is great. If not, the guy is finished. If it rains, it's the superintendent's fault." Further, he was criticized for "shuffling" people around "constantly."[85] The motivation for these movements, from Hartzog's perspective, was both organizational and personal, i. e. individual development through new challenges. In the view of the long-time, less-valued folk, the shifts were likely seen as Hartzog making the organization in his own image.

Recognizing the Contradictions

There can be no doubt that such tensions existed in the Hartzog era; and it is a source of bafflement to specify what Hartzog might have done differently. As a personality, he was an extremely powerful, dominant person. As an idealist, he had clear, strongly-held views about the parks and their purposes. If he had not honored himself and his ideals, he could not have achieved what he did. Further, he was a person who could handle and indeed welcome feedback. He thrived on confrontation, from which he thought a resolution was likely best to reflect the community interest.

Hierarchical Values as the Culprit

Any inadequacies in the human system of the Park Service should likely not be charged to Hartzog. The real difficulty lies in a commitment to hierarchical values that inhibited subordinates from communicating cleanly and openly with the boss. Such norms are deeply embedded in the Service; it is probably fair to say that most of its leaders got along by going along. Hartzog had trouble getting even his top staff to free themselves from their bureaucratic experiences and to reach out in new directions. They, in effect, allowed him to usurp more power than Hartzog himself thought was good for the organization.

Given some of the difficulties identified above, Hartzog struggled diligently to make the Park Service an exciting, creative place in which individuals would have an opportunity to use themselves fully. He was determined not to make the mistake he felt Conrad Wirth had committed with him. He did go to the parks. He did know what was going on. He talked to his people to learn of their needs and aspirations. And he was always looking for good people. As he has commented, "I was always recruiting. I was convinced that the Park Service was too rigid and inflexible. If you didn't become Director, you left. And if you left, you were through. I resolved that we were going to loosen up the system and bring in people from outside at various grade levels."[86]

The Hartzog experience suggests the many difficulties, indeed contradictions, that attend any effort to appraise managerial performance. Certainly it can be said that Hartzog was a dedicated manager. Further, he recognized that the quality and motivation of his people were critical to organization success. Yet these concerns had to be articulated within a framework of organization imperatives largely defined by the leader in his relationships with a larger environment. Fundamentally, Hartzog's profound commitment to the goals of the Park Service brought him into collision either with people who did not share those aspirations or who were unable to contribute in full measure to their accomplishment. A manager who faces up to such realities will undoubtedly deliver hard news, will engage in major surgery on the staff through dismissals and unexpected promotions, and will deliberately excite uncertainty as he seeks to pull the organization away from its "steady state" orientations. It is interesting that these behaviors seemed of necessity to co-exist with an almost Maslovian desire on Hartzog's part to make the Park Service a place where people could reach the peak experience of using themselves fully. The aspiration to achieve both organizational and personal gratification should not be regarded as totally unrealistic, but the Hartzog experience suggests there is no easy way, even for the best of leaders, to achieve total success on both sides.

The Post-Departure Experience

Generally, when one departs an employment situation, the relationship is perceived as having been concluded. The break is typically regarded as a clean one. Not so in the public service, particularly for those who have occupied high-level positions. For a variety of political and personal reasons, old antagonisms persist. The period after public service can often prove exceedingly vexing and stressful. No matter how scrupulous a person seeks to be in the conduct of government responsibilities, the possibility of harassment always exists. That certainly was the experience of George Hartzog. In considerable degree he regarded it as the most negative aspect of public service.

Assaults on His Reputation

There were several different assaults on his reputation and on his pocketbook. The costs were five years of time spent in defending himself and the expenditure of tens of thousands of dollars in lawyer's fees and other burdens associated with his defense. The general allegations were that he represented a client who had a conflict of interest, that he had accepted bribes and kickbacks in the award of architectural contracts, and that he had used government lodging without paying for it. In addition to the FBI and the department's auditors, the bribery and kickback accusations occasioned the attention of the Internal Revenue Service, which was checking to see whether he had reported all of his alleged ill-gotten gains.

Audit by the Internal Revenue Service

As many citizens know, a full audit by IRS is an excruciating event. Hartzog signed a waiver of the statute of limitations; and the investigation went back more than 10 years to the time when he had become superintendent in St. Louis. The investigation quickly got away from conflict of interest gains and focused on a house his wife had purchased as an investment in California. She had deducted the cost of a trip to California to handle matters pertaining to the property; but the IRS insisted her sole purpose was to visit her daughter. The investigation, which lasted more than 10 years, resulted in a $400 levy on a travel expenditure which Hartzog's own accountants still contend was fully legitimate.

Conflict of Interest Charges

Conflict of interest allegations prompted an investigation by the Criminal Division of the Justice Department. In this case Hartzog was accused of serving as an attorney in 1974 on the renewal of a contract which he had originally awarded as Director.[87] As an attorney he was prohibited from having any participation in a matter in which he had been involved as a government official. In reality the contract had been awarded at a much lower level in the organization; and, after a year's investigation, Richard L. Thornburgh, then the Assistant Attorney General, declared the case closed. In a letter dated March 1, 1976, he wrote that there was "...insufficient evidence to support any allegation."[88]

The Mardirosian Case

But Hartzog's troubles were not over. About two months after the Thornburgh letter, the *Washington Post* (June 16, 1976) reported that the American Institute of Architects was investigating allegations that a former National Park Service architect, Aram Mardirosian, had engaged in unprofessional conduct. Essentially, Mardirosian was charged with criticizing another architect's work on the National Visitors' Center in Washington, D. C., for personal gain. As a result, it was alleged that he had been able to secure a $600,000 contract for himself from the Park Service. The *Post* mistakenly declared that the contract was negotiated in 1972, when Hartzog was still in office, and implied the event occurred on the Hartzog watch. The award was actually made in 1973.

This case demonstrates how public responsibilities do not have neat cutoffs with employment termination. Even if the *Post* had given the right date for the $600,000 contract award, Hartzog would still have been brought into the situation. On November 11, 1976, the *Post* reported, "The FBI is investigating $600,000 worth of National Park Service contracts awarded between 1970 and 1975 to Washington architect, Aram Mardirosian... Sources familiar with the investigation said its scope includes Mardirosian's relationship with former Park Service Director George Hartzog...." What had occurred was that Hartzog had hired Mardirosian as Artist-in-Residence in 1969. He recalled in a statement to an FBI investigator:

> The Artist-in-Residence for the NPS was less than a full time position. I helped create the position when Secretary Udall was head of

the U. S. Department of the Interior…It was set up [in the sixties] in order to attract artists, professionals, and talented individuals in order to critique the NPS in design and communications systems for our projects. The Artists-in-Residence program was used to improve the whole quality of our projects and to bring in an outside viewpoint. My first meeting with Mardirosian must have been during 1967 or 1968 after this position was created. The reason for the creation of the position was that the NPS had a critical problem of design of public buildings.[89]

Mardirosian was hired on a one year contract, which was subsequently renewed. At about the time he was completing his assignment, the Park Service was struggling to find a suitable architect for the Museum of Westward Expansion in St. Louis. The Gateway Arch had been finished in 1965; but the Museum was far from completed five years later. As the Assistant Director of the Park Service reported in a memo in 1970, a number of prominent architects had been contacted and would not take the assignment. It was at that time that Mardirosian, identified as the chief of design of the Potomac Group, was proposed. He was awarded a contract of $280,000 for the design, 16 days after he departed his Park Service assignment, which had never been full-time. It is true, of course, that government employees are prohibited from receiving any contracts until they have been out of the service for a year. If the law was violated, many people at many levels were involved. Hartzog represented only one step in the chain of approvals, which went well above him.

What seemed particularly to interest the FBI was a "Follow-up Slip," written by Assistant Director William Everhart, in which he noted that the Potomac Group did "not officially exist" [It was being created by Mardirosian at the time.] and that Hartzog had suggested Mardrosian's name not be used in a request for authorization to go outside the Park Service for architectual services.[90] The issue was going outside, not selecting an architect. As Hartzog pointed out in another statement to the FBI (April 5, 1977), the elaborate contracting process of the Department of the Interior must be understood. It requires the Park Service to secure higher authority approval to go outside in the first place and then to receive subsequent approval to hire a specific person. His own view was that, "…Mardirosian was no longer connected with the National Park Service; therefore, in my mind, no conflict of interest situation existed."[91]

Continuing Harassment

Still, at the same time the FBI was declaring Hartzog was not the target of an investigation, he was hearing from friends that FBI agents were raising questions about him. One former associate in Arkansas wrote that he had been asked, "Do you know or have you ever heard of kickbacks being taken by George Hartzog during the time he was Director of the National Park Service?" The former associate said he responded in a "profane manner since I know you so well and know that you would shoot your best friend before you would take a kickback from him."[92]

The FBI, for reasons that have not been satisfactorily explained, was in no mood to retreat. An official response came to Hartzog's lawyers on June 24, 1977 that "Mr. Hartzog was not a target of this investigation." Yet a later sentence says, "…there was some evidence that Mr. Hartzog was aware of a possible conflict of interest in appointing an employee of the National Park Service (Mardirosian) to be recipient of a National Park Service contract."[93] In response to another representation from Hartzog's lawyers, the FBI again made the point that the former Director was "aware of a possible conflict of interest." It continued, "…among the documents which gave rise to this investigation was a memorandum between two high level Park Service employees which stated that the 'Potomac Group' did not officially exist and George Hartzog suggested we do not mention Aram's (Mardirosian) name."[94] The writer of the cited memo, William Everhart, had said that he was simply making bureaucratic points; Hartzog's cited comment did not in any way imply cover-up.

Department of Interior Audit of Lodging Arrangements

Meanwhile, on a visit to a deputy Assistant Secretary of Interior, Hartzog learned that the Department's auditors had been investigating visits he had made to Fort Jefferson, in Florida, in the time he was Director and in the year after he had left office. The Park Service has a number of facilities with lodging, such as at Fort Jefferson, and the charge was that Hartzog had stayed free both when Director and afterwards. Further, he had provided free lodging to others. There was no basis for the accusations. He had always paid for himself; and, on rare occasions when members of Congress failed to reimburse the government, he had written a personal check. The auditors found nothing.

Unseen, Unknown Accusers

In the same meeting with the deputy assistant Secretary, Hartzog also learned of the official's attendance at a session where someone had raised the question of the former Director's having received kickbacks from Mardirosian. The deputy Assistant Secretary revealed at a later luncheon that his own review of the investigations of Hartzog, reported by Hartzog, "...indicated that someone in the Department had definitely been harassing me since my departure."[95]

In a May 23, 1977 letter, Thomas H. Henderson, Jr., Chief, Public Integrity Section of the Department of Justice, advised the Solicitor of the Department of Interior that, "...based upon the information currently in our possession we have concluded that an indictable case has not been established and we decline prosecution."[96] Notwithstanding, it appears that there was no real closure to the FBI investigation. In June, 1977, a letter was addressed to the FBI pointing out that the investigation was doing great harm to Hartzog's reputation. A response was requested that made clear Hartzog had violated no laws and was not under investigation. No such "unambigious" reply was received. On December 22, 1977, Hartzog's attorney addressed another letter to the FBI. Certain clarifying points were again made, and he concluded, "Having failed on two prior occasions to receive an unqualified response to our specific request, we are submitting this letter for the record only.[97] Some vindication of Hartzog occurred, however, when architect Mardirosian was awarded $750,000 damages in a law suit against the American Institute of Architects.

It is interesting that Hartzog was able to wage a successful defense because of lessons learned from the McCarthyism of the fifties. He has written:

> Early in my public career I observed portions of the McCarthy hearings...One of the many people Senator McCarthy attempted to smear with his "Soft on Communism" brush was Methodist Bishop G. Bromley Oxnam. Based on his meticulous log of every meeting, every trip and of every organization of which he was a member, Bishop Oxnam demolished the reckless allegations of the Senator. Then and there I resolved to keep a daily log—every telephone call, meeting and trip. The habit became so ingrained that even today I never pick up the telephone unless I have my log and

a pencil at hand. From the beginning of our marriage of more than 40 years I have kept every bank statement, cancelled check, check book and paid bill…One FBI agent remarked after observing my documentation, "I have never seen anything like this in my life."[98]

Hartzog observed that he had played "hardball" all of his public life and liked the game. But this was "dirty ball." He reported a particularly poignant moment when he found his 13-year-old son weeping. He asked the reason for the tears as he put his arms around him. The boy blurted, "Because you are going to jail!" Hartzog writes, "Father and son wept together—he in his concern for me; me in my fury and frustration over how much he was hurting."[99]

Public Integrity as a Masquerade for Personal, Political Vendettas

While public officials must be held to high ethical standards, the Hartzog case suggests how such an expectation can be turned and used against former officials, irrespective of their records for integrity. Personal and political vendettas can masquerade as efforts to protect the public interest. Hartzog never did discover for certain who his accusers were, but the pattern of behavior was familiar. There were harassing accusations that took money and time to refute. Further, the agencies of both government and the media were mobilized to press the vendetta. The continued interest of the FBI in the case, for example, was considered to be occasioned more by the report in the *Washington Post* that Hartzog was under investigation than by the inter-office memorandum which was constantly cited. Thus both the FBI and the *Post* were enlisted to make life thoroughly miserable for an eminent and responsible public official.

Conclusion

While it is apparent that George Hartzog has genes abundantly endowed with intelligence and energy, his status as a *great* Director of the National Park Service rests more significantly on a value system that has motivated and directed him to personal and organizational accomplishment. That value system tends to have three basic components: (a) personal integrity; (b) democratic conviction, with all attendant beliefs in popular sovereignty; and (c) religion.

Hartzog was born and raised in a small town in rural South Carolina. It is the norms of that place and time that shaped and defined Hartzog as a person. He has commented:

> I grew up with the values of the South. A man's word is his bond. My mother's father was a Civil War veteran. He always borrowed money from the bank for spring planting and fertilizing. Never in his life did he sign a note. Even if his family suffered, money was paid back on time because his word was his bond. My credo when I became the Park Service Director, with all the political pressures, was a little bit different. It was to promise slowly and perform promptly.[100]

Hartzog's family knew difficult economic times; but these experiences only emphasized the importance of valuing one's self and taking full advantage of one's resources to meet the challenge. His father farmed land that had been in the family for generations, with a satisfactory income before the depression. When the price of cotton dropped to five cents per pound and watermelons did not even cover the cost of their freight, the family plight was desperate. As Hartzog has put it, "For a dirt farmer who had been put out of business, life became a very simple issue: Did we have something to eat or didn't we…? This was the poverty level of zero."[101] The father became a severe asthmatic; and, in the same period, the family house burned down. It is in the context of these overwhelming problems that Hartzog saw his mother as the anchor, the rock that kept the family together. She simply did not give up.

Although his family was critical to Hartzog's development, the community of Walterboro seemed to provide him remarkable opportunities for growth. He began preaching when he was sixteen and received a license in the following year, 1937. In high school he learned shorthand and took maximum advantage of this skill, traveling the political circuit and recording the verbatim statements of candidates in the various campaigns. Very early, he made friends with some of the most important people in the state. The business people of Walterboro thought so much of him that they provided money for him to go to Wofford College. Because his support was needed by the family, he was not able to stay in school. At the age of 19, he went to work in a local law office as a stenographer, was given the opportunity to read the law, and 33 months later took and passed the bar examinations of South Carolina.[102] Thus there seemed to be a remarkable melding of Hartzog capacities and a hospitable, receptive environment.

Only a few moments of conversation will quickly reveal his deep commitment to the U. S. political system. He is utterly attached to it, adores its frailties, and can think of nothing more delightful than participating in it. If his wife [a Bostonian] had been willing to live in the South, he undoubtedly would have pursued a political career. Shortly before he was to be married, an offer was made to him to finance his campaign for the South Carolina House of Representatives. As he recounted the incident, it is clear that Hartzog still savored the idea of a vigorous political campaign. The recollection also brings forth memories of the South Carolina culture that produced such a strong commitment to the American political system:

> I was fortunate in going to work for Joe Moorer. He and his partner, Colonel Padgett, had been in the South Carolina legislature for years. Moorer's brother-in-law was old Senator "Cotton Ed" Smith, who was an inspiration despite my differences with his political ideas…I traveled with him as he went from precinct to precinct…I also got to know Senator Jimmy Byrnes as a young fellow and was hired to take down his speeches. He also became somewhat of a model for me.[103]

There can be no doubt that Hartzog's belief in, and enthusiasm for, the American political process made him a special and rather unique bureaucratic leader.

While the political system was his secular religion, Hartzog never moved away from his profound moorings in the Methodist church. He is an exceedingly devout person who still talks of his original ambition to be a clergyman. Some measure of his religious commitment is to be seen in the fact that he has tithed throughout his working life. It has occurred even when he has been personally in debt. When asked whether he could afford to tithe under such circumstances, he said he had no option. The money did not belong to him. It belonged to the Lord.

Hartzog frames much of his language and description of his activities in terms of the pastorate. He saw his job as Director of the Park Service as a mission, not very different from the work of the church. As a youngster coming up with an ambition to go into the ministry, he had a commitment to serve other people."The thing that pulls you into the public service and keeps you there is that same interest in serving people."[104] He speaks of converting people to the causes in which he has invested deeply."I am not trying to make people Methodist. But I am trying to get them to recognize the public interest. When you are dealing with the logging industry, you are trying to convert them, not to a faith but to a cause. You are seeking some kind of compromise that meets their needs and also serves the public interest."

Religion is a very personal and private matter for George Hartzog. On the job it is never discussed. Indeed, he is sufficiently profane and irreverent as to suggest little attachment to any church. He emphasizes that religion does not enter into his work at the conscious level. Instead, it functions very much as an internal beacon."Religion impacts you as a person; and you impact the Park Service as a person," he says."I could no more steal now as a practicing lawyer than when I was Director because I believe very deeply that stealing is not an acceptable method of living, based on my understanding of the Ten Commandments, in the Judeo-Christian tradition."[105] Such a strong religious belief undoubtedly accounted for much of the commitment, drive, and selfless effort that have characterized George B. Hartzog, Jr. and brought the National Park Service to a peak of performance.

Notes

1. Material in this section was orignially published in Terry L. Cooper and N. Dale Wright, eds., *Exemplary Public Administrators: Character and Leadership in Government*. San Francisco; Jossey-Bass, 1992, 130–165.
2. *The National Parks: Shaping the System* (Washington, D. C. : Division of Publications, National Park Service, Department of the Interior, 1985), 62.
3. John McPhee, "Profile: G. Hartzog," *New Yorker* 45: 48 (September 11, 1971), 45–6.
4. Bill Connelly, "GOP, Ecology Headhunters Finally Get Park Director," *Richmond Times Dispatch*, December 10, 1972. The official number was 69.
5. Editorial, *Washington Evening Star*, December 15, 1972. Again, the official number was 69.
6. *Shaping the System*, 62.
7. *Loc. cit.*
8. *Loc. cit.*
9. *Ibid.*, 72.

10. This profile is very likely one of the very few *The New Yorker* has ever published of a practicing bureaucrat.
11. *Ibid.*, 48.
12. William C. Everhart, *The National Park Service* (Boulder, Colorado: Westview Press, 1983), 27.
13. *Loc. cit.*
14 Brent Breedin, "George Hartzog Steps Down from National Park Post," *The State*, probably December 10, 1972.
15. Everhart, 151.
16. *Ibid.*, 28.
17. *Ibid.*, 150.
18. *Ibid*, 28.
19. George B. Hartzog, *Battling for the National Parks* (Mt. Kisco, NY: Moyer Bell, Ltd., 1988), 243–7.
20. Everhart, 151.
21. Hartzog, 241.
22. Editorial, *Washington Evening Star*, December 15, 1972.
23. Editorial, *St. Louis Post-Dispatch*, December 12, 1972.
24. Letter, Donald Hodel, Secretary of the Interior, to George B. Hartzog, Jr., May 3, 1985.
25. Letter, Roy Taylor to George B. Hartzog, Jr., no date.
26. Letter, William A. Turnage, President, The Wilderness Society, to George B. Hartzog, Jr., May 8, 1985.
27. Letters to Hartzog Concerning the Dedication of the JNEM Visistors Center, File 66, Box 8A, Series 4, MSS74. Special Collections, Clemson University Libraries, Clemson, SC.
28. Hartzog, xi–xiv.
29. Letter, Wallace Stegner to Brett Bell [Moyer-Bell, Inc.], February 26, 1988. File 7, Box 2, Series 3, MSS74. Special Collections, Clemson University Libraries, Clemson, SC.
30. Conrad L. Wirth, *Parks, Politics, and the People* (Norman, Oklahoma: University of Oklahoma Press, 1980), 304.
31. Hartzog, 76.
32. *Ibid.*, 39.
33. McPhee, 52.
34. *Ibid.*, 78.
35. *Ibid.*, 80.
36. Wirth, 297–301.
37. Hartzog, 86–8.
38. Everhart, 26.
39. Wirth, 300–11.
40. Wirth, 301–3.
41. Hartzog, 74.
42. *Ibid.*, 74–5.
43. McPhee, 80.

44. Hartzog, 75.
45. *Ibid.*, 76.
46. Hartzog, 77–8.
47. *Ibid.*, 77
48. Wirth, 301
49. Ibid., 312
50. McPhee, 82.
51. Harlan Cleveland, *The Future Executive: A Guide for Tomorrow's Managers* (New York: Harper and Row, 1972). See Chapter 6, 75ff.
52. Letter, Howard Baker to Jerry Schober, March 25, 1985.
53. McPhee, 68.
54. Connelly, December 10, 1972.
55. Hartzog, 6.
56. *Ibid.*, 10.
57. Editorial, *The Kemmerer Gazette*, Kemmerer Wyoming, March 30, 1972.
58. McPhee, 60.
59. *Ibid.*, 87.
60. "Morton Backs Hartzog in Park Controversy," *Parks and Recreation*, September 1, 1972, 49.
61. *Ibid.*, 50.
62. Editorial, *Washington Post*, December 12, 1972.
63. Robert Cahn, "Hartzog Leaves Legacy of Goals for Parks," *Christian Science Monitor*, December 23, 1972.
64. Hartzog, 79. He reports that Dr. Stanley Cain, a former Interior Assistant Secretary, is responsible for the characterization.
65. *Ibid.*, 80.
66. McPhee, 45.
67. *Ibid.*, 48–9.
68. Hartzog, "Introduction," xiii.
69. McPhee, 60.
70. *Loc. cit.*
71. Warren Bennis and Burt Nanus, *Leaders: The Strategies for Taking Charge* (New York: Harper and Row, 1985), paper, 101.
72. McPhee, 67.
73. *Ibid.*, 59.
74. *Ibid.*, 60.
75. Hartzog, 189.
76. McPhee, 70.
77. *Loc. cit.*
78. *Ibid.*, 67.
79. *Loc. cit.*
80. *Ibid.*, 68.
81. *Loc. cit.*
82. Interview with George B. Hartzog, Jr., McLean, Virginia, November 8, 1989.
83. *Loc. cit.*

84. McPhee, 62
85. *Ibid.*, 60
86. Frank P. Sherwood, "George B. Hartzog, Jr. : Career Bureaucrat Who Made A Difference—And Wrote About It," *Federal Management* 1:19 (Fall, 1988).
87. Letter from Agent Lindgren, Dec. 31, 1974. File 13, Box 2, Series 4, MSS 74. Special Collections, Clemson University Libraries.
88. Letter from Richard L. Thornburgh, March, 1, 1976. File 15, Box 2, Series 4, MSS 74. Special Collections, Clemson University Libraries.
89. Statment to the FBI, March 20, 1977. File 12, Box 2, Series 4, MSS 74. Special Collections, Clemson University Libraries.
90. "Follow-up Slip to Joe Jensen," June 12, 1970, Exhibit 7. File 12, Box 2, Series 4, MSS 74. Special Collections, Clemson University Libraries.
91. Statement, April 5, 1977. File 12, Box 2, Series 4, MSS 74. Special Collections, Clemson University Libraries.
92. Letter, Ivan Parker, Personnel Manager, Department of Parks and Tourism, State of Arkansas, to George Hartzog, May 12, 1977.
93. File 12, Box 2, Series 4, MSS 74. Special Collections, Clemson University Libraries.
94. Letter, Thomas W. Henderson, Jr., Chief Public Integrity Section, Criminal Division, Federal Bureau of Investigation, to Andrew A. Normandeau, Sept. 9, 1977. File 12, Box 2, Series 4, MSS 74. Special Collections, Clemson University Libraries.
95. Memorandum, George Hartzog to Andrew A. Normandeau, September 27, 1977. File 12, Box 2, Series 4, MSS 74. Special Collections, Clemson University Libraries.
96. Letter, Thomas H. Henderson, Jr., to Leo Krulitz, Solicitor, Department of Interior, May 12, 1977. File 12, Box 2, Series 4, MSS 74. Special Collections, Clemson University Libraries.
97. Letter, Andrew A. Normandeau to Thomas H. Henderson, December 22, 1977. File 12, Box 2, Series 4, MSS 74. Special Collections, Clemson University Libraries.
98. Written statement by George B. Hartzog, Jr., undated, 3 pages. File 12, Box 2, Series 4, MSS 74. Special Collections, Clemson University Libraries.
99. *Ibid.*, 2.
100. Interview, November 8, 1989.
101. McPhee, 74.
102. Hartzog, 16–20.
103. Interview, November 8, 1989.
104. *Loc. cit.*
105. *Loc. cit.*

Chapter Four

GEORGE B. HARTZOG, JR.:
LEADER—EXECUTIVE—MANAGER

by Frank P. Sherwood

George B Hartzog, Jr. and I first encountered each other at the opening of the Federal Executive Institute in Charlottesville, Virginia, in October, 1968. By that time he had already been Director of the National Park Service for more than four years, and still he had enrolled in the first session of a new enterprise charged with the development and support of the roughly 10,000 at the top of the Federal career service. In those days they were called the "Supergrades" in the classified service, and we gave them the additional title of executives.

But George was of an even higher status. He was a Level Five among the leaders in the Federal government, who were above the Supergrades. I was the Director of the fledgling Institute and was pleased, and also anxious, that someone of George's status would decide to join us. But he was only one case for concern. We had enough worries with meeting the needs of the Supergrades, let alone one of their bosses.

George quickly set us at ease, as those who know him would have expected. At the very outset he was his usual friendly self, expressed a lot of enthusiasm for the learning he expected to experience, and really infected others with his obvious confidence that the FEI was going to be a great place to take a fresh look at life and work.

It was my first brush with George Hartzog, and I certainly liked what I saw. Later I came to understand that what I was experiencing was the genuine George. Here was a man who was willing to take risks in the pursuit of personal development. His outlook was one of optimism, with the result that he was happy to give us a chance to show him that we had something to offer. And he was curious. He liked the interagency complexion of the place and was enthused about learning from his colleagues. There was no pretense; here was a man who clearly loved human interaction and wanted it to be as warm and real as possible.

George was a key individual in that group of 65 highly graded officers of the government who helped me negotiate a very rough road for this new and unique undertaking. I have thought many times about that first difficult night and the unseen help he gave me.

There was one other aspect of those early days. We recognized, quite correctly, that the 10,000 people at the top (almost all of whom were men) would have varying degrees of preparation for the jobs they were occupying. Many had advanced academic degrees, but often with little relevance to the kinds of leadership roles they were playing. George was one of the rare ones. He had high qualifications, was a practicing attorney, had received a bachelor's degree in business administration at American University, and had completed nearly all the requirements for his MBA there.

To meet the diverse needs of the 65 participants, we offered a wide range of courses in that first session. The one I provided was about as impractical and unapplied as you could get, "The Pure Theory of Organization." Guess who signed up enthusiastically? George Hartzog! He was one of six to do so.

As it turned out, we did not see nearly as much of George Hartzog in October and November 1968 as we would have liked. He was absent from classes at least one-third of the time, and the reason was Lady Bird Johnson, the first Lady. She was the great supporter of the parks, and she expected George to be present whenever she appeared. Since her schedule involved many trips to the parks, George had to be with her. There can be no doubt that their close and warm collaboration operated very much to foster the growth and development of the parks.

George saw enough of the Federal Executive Institute that he became one of our most major supporters. He made sure that all his top staff attended; and I do not believe there was another Federal agency where the FEI had such presence. He also proposed rather early to the FEI National Advisory Board that a model consulting relationship be established, with the Park Service footing the bill. Finally, he volunteered to have Park Service experts review our communications to be sure they reflected the FEI commitment to change, a goal we saw as central to our mission. No one was a greater believer in the FEI and its purposes than George Hartzog.

George Hartzog as a Personal Friend and as a Federal Executive

While the Federal Executive Institute was a very small part in the eventful Hartzog life, it has a particular place in this chapter. It was the place where we met and cemented a warm relationship that persisted over

40 years. It is the way in which I came to know a truly remarkable man, and about whom I feel the imperative to add some personal feelings and insights to the many words that have already been written about him. In considerable degree this is a memoir that I feel is necessary to write. George was like only a few special people in my life, for whom I have had great affection and profound respect. I have needed to write about them to bring my deep feelings for them to a kind of closure.

There is, however, another reason for this chapter. It is even more specifically related to the Federal Executive Institute. Around the time George passed away in 2008, I was already at work on a book, which was later titled, *The Early Years of the Federal Executive Institute*.[1] It was published in 2010 and records the history of about a decade of effort to provide development and support to the Federal Government's top career executives. While the FEI continues at the same location in Charlottesville, its mission is now to provide residential training for upper middle managers in the government. It has less concern for those at the very top.

It has long been my conviction that the cause of effective government suffered a major blow when the FEI's original charter was withdrawn and it became a management training center. As I speculated over the reasons for the absence of support for the FEI and its original mission, it became apparent that there were relatively few who really believed there were true executives in the career service of the Federal government. I learned early that there were many such executives, but sadly I was unable to convey that reality to key decision-makers. As I contemplated the case of the unrecognized executives in writing the book, my thoughts often turned to George Hartzog. Here was the person, more than anyone else, who typified the Federal career executive for me. It may be a little late in the process to seek now to convince people that George—and many others like him—were real, but it gives me some satisfaction to record the types of behaviors and attributes that made him an outstanding executive. I first encountered George as an executive and never lost that image of him.

Down to the Bare Essentials: Early and Late Life

It has long been my contention that the behavior you see coming from an office in an organization is the result of two factors: (a) the personal attributes of the person occupying the top position and (b) the expectations directed to that position from the many forces in the environment relating to that position. Within this context, even George Hartzog was not entirely his own man in the National Park Service. In order to see what he brought to the situation, we have to look beyond his public persona. His wife of 61 years, his dear Helen, and his three children undoubtedly know him as no one else does. As is to be expected, those of us outside that small family circle have to find other ways to define the "real" George Hartzog.

My own sense is that the early and late days in the life of a person tend to reveal his/her essence. I, of course, did not know George when he was young, but I did have a fairly close association with him when he was aging and not in particularly good health.

Hartzog: Finding Jobs When No One Else Could

There is one way, however, in which I feel reasonably close to George as a young man. We were both born in the same year, 1920, and so I am very much aware of the difficult economic times through which almost all of us went in the 1920s and 1930s. We grew up on opposite coasts; but, as I read George's arresting stories of survival in South Carolina, they do not seem dramatically different from the times I experienced in San Diego, California. It cannot be denied, of course, that George's life was tougher than mine; yet I have a very strong awareness of what he was going through, something that later generations could never possibly understand.

What is most impressive is the whirlwind of activity in which he engaged from the time he left high school at age 16 until he was drafted on his 23rd birthday. He lived in a small South Carolina town, Walterboro, in which I would guess jobs were even scarcer than in San Diego. My count from his book is that he held six different jobs in about two years. The first two were as a gas station attendant during the day and a clerk at a hotel at night. After leaving college after one semester, he held positions on a bread truck, as a clerk for the National Youth Administration, as a clerk in the county welfare department, and as a secretary in a law office.[2] It is hard for me to believe that anyone could have landed so many jobs in those very difficult times. George must have been attractive and aggressive, far beyond anything I or my many job-seeking friends could even imagine.

A second feature of those youthful times was his drive for personal growth. It is simply amazing to me that he took typing and stenography in high school.³ I don't remember a boy at my high school who took typing, much less stenography. Yet I am sure those competences made some of George's jobs possible. And then there was reading the law, starting at age 19 and culminating with passing the bar at age 22. Even in those days, it was very rare for someone to engage in legal studies as George did. Further, the whole process required extreme persistence. It was only on the third try that he passed the bar.⁴

It is difficult to know how to categorize a third career accomplishment—his licensure as a local minister in Walterboro. As he wrote, "My mother and dad shared with me their love and pride in their church. Encouraged by them it was my ambition to become a Methodist preacher. In the summer of 1937 (he was 17) I was licensed by the Methodist church as a local preacher—the youngest one in the state at that time."⁵ This was a mooring that never left him and demanded of him a high degree of ethics in all of his dealings.

One thing I have learned from the Federal Executive Institute is that many people, even those who gain topmost positions, see life as a lonely journey. They do not view other people as particularly friendly and certainly not as helpers. Valuing others for their friendship and their willingness to be helpful is the mark of a confident, warm person. George seems early to have understood the importance of friendships and their potential for providing support. It was a friend of his parents, the owner of a military academy, who insisted George attend his institution free and get his high school degree. A group of local businessmen financed a semester's attendance at Wofford College. It was Joe Moorer, a Walterboro attorney, who agreed to guide George through the three years of intensive studies in preparation for his qualification as a practicing attorney.⁶ And he became good friends with Paul H. Gantt, a fellow lawyer he met when first drafted into the Army. He contacted Gantt after his Army discharge and received his help in securing his first government job.⁷

Hartzog was a fast learner and much of the behavior that served him so well in later life was likely impressed on him in the early years. He writes of the campaign strategy of his dear friend, Dick Jeffries:

> At every campaign stop, or 'stump speakin', the first thing Dick Jeffries would do was head straight for Colonel Pearcy [his opponent] and the group of people around him. He would push his way in, shake hands with the Colonel first and then work the crowd. One

day after the speeches were over and the crowd was breaking up, an old farmer, who had observed Jeffries' performance on several occasions, said to Colonel Pearcy, "Winston, if you are so much opposed to Dick Jeffries, why are you always shakin' hands with him?"[8]

Hartzog himself answered the old man's question by noting that Jeffries won the election handily, and then proceeded to explain the lesson the experience had provided: "On the campaign trail with Colonel Pearcy, Dick Jeffries taught me that if pressin' the flesh of your adversaries doesn't convert them, it sure disarms them and confuses the bystanders."[9]

Three Years in the Army: An Uncommonly Impressive Performance

George Hartzog was drafted into the Army in the Spring, 1943, a few months ahead of me (my service began in September of that year). It was an unusual time. The government had done a really spectacular job of mobilizing troops for a war that was sure to escalate. By 1943, however, just about everyone was in place, and recruits were assigned one role: to serve as cannon fodder. Virtually all hands went to infantry training camps.

But George Hartzog did not. It is highly probable that his status as a practicing attorney led to his assignment as a clerk in the Judge Advocate General Corps. But that particular qualification doesn't explain his later assignment to officers' training in the Transportation Corps and his even later service as an officer in the Military Police.[10] We have to look for a further explanation why George did not join the rest of us in the infantry.

The Army in 1943 was, in substantial degree, a meritocracy. It was a very different deal from 1942, when a number of people of modest capacity were given significant responsibility. A year or so later the Army could be extremely choosy—and it was. The few who met the Army's exacting standards for leadership were identified and protected by the system. My suspicion is that George Hartzog was one of those chosen few.

What was it about George Hartzog that made him stand out? In this analysis I will compare him to another friend, a fraternity brother who was at the same basic infantry training camp as I. Bill was there because a special Army program was cancelled. He was physically impressive, an attractive human being, highly adept at all the things you had to do in the Army, and able to accept the ways in which the Army infringes on an individual's life. Indeed, it was more than acceptance; he did his level best to honor all the expectations directed toward him. His reward was an offer to stay at the camp as a trainer, rather than to be shipped off to the South Pacific. That the Army was right in its judgment is evident in his later development of a large and highly successful business in Cincinnati.

My guess is that George Hartzog was another "Bill" and attracted similar attention from his superiors. By age 23 he was likely fully grown, an imposing figure of more than average height, good looking and clean cut, with military bearing. There is little doubt that he was charismatic, a dominating figure in any group of soldiers, and with a command presence. It is important, and rightly so, that the Army looked for people who had an almost automatic followership. It's probable, too, that George experienced little difficulty in mastering the various competences that are seen as vital in military leadership: excellent marksmanship, complete ease in close order drill, and a hearty voice to bark out commands. Finally, he had to be a person who thought quickly on his feet; and, as we know from his later life, George was seldom at a loss in dealing with new and quickly developing situations. Those who knew George in his leadership years in the Park Service will not find these descriptors of him surprising. It is only noteworthy that they were present early in his life. Given the very few opportunities available to draftees in 1943, I believe we have to look to these special qualities to understand how he received a commission and had a relatively successful military career. And I believe my situation as a fellow soldier has allowed me to recognize the assets that led to his above average success in an Army that was overwhelmed in 1943 with young, very able men.

An Aging George Hartzog: Much the Same

George Hartzog led a highly active, thoroughly energetic life. I don't believe he restricted himself in any way. That produced many accomplishments, as he expended the "animal-like energies," which Harlan Cleveland saw in successful executives. There is the down side, however—namely that the parts of our complex body can't handle the workload. We are often left with many years of ill health, which we handle in various ways.

For most of the last two decades of his life, George suffered a serious onslaught of Type II Diabetes. It affected his health in many ways, but most importantly it forced the amputation of his left leg below the knee. Excess weight, extreme soreness at the amputation site, and a prosthesis that never seemed to fit properly left him permanently consigned to a wheelchair. A very large room [at least 600 square feet] with great open windows was constructed at the rear of the Hartzog's colonial house in McLean. The room allowed as much of a feeling of being outdoors as was possible within a structure; but it was within this single space that George lived for many years. It was here that I spent enjoyable hours with George, often also with Helen and Susie [my wife].

One cannot write about George in old age without including Helen. Throughout his illness she was essentially his sole caregiver. When I saw her, she occasionally looked very tired but never dejected. She ministered to George's many needs with tremendous dedication and extremely good spirit, even when a shelf of shoes fell on her in a department store and virtually crippled her. As she lamely moved around, her good spirit dominated. I don't believe George was ever made to feel he was a burden.

Within this setting, what could I tell about the elements of his character that persisted without the trappings of office and symbols of status? Religious affiliations could be one indication of his basic quality, but that is risky. Many profess religion but do not act it. In George's case the Methodist religion was deep in his South Carolina roots, and the commitment to its values was very real. That's important because there is nothing so critical to true leadership as integrity. I never heard of anyone who questioned George's.

Religion, however, was a very private matter for him. You can put the puzzle together only with scraps of information. He wrote on several occasions of his commitment to the Judeo-Christian ethic, and he provided a Down South illustration, in which his grandfather borrowed money from the bank for his annual plantings but never signed a note. A handshake reflected full commitment to the obligation.

George's deep loyalty to the Methodist Church as an institution was well-established by age 17 when he was first licensed to preach. He tithed regularly throughout his life. And it was striking that he took very seriously the proper burial of his family. There is a lovely cemetery in Walterboro, in ways both primitive and elegantly designed, in which he began buying burial plots many years ago. He had his parents moved there, and that is where he rests today. Helen reported recently that she still owns about 20 plots in that cemetery. In our many conversations, George mentioned the cemetery several times. It was obviously very important him.

The closest we came to a full-blown discussion of religion was one in which he expressed the somewhat surprising view that there is nothing sacred about the body. It will indeed return to dust. But he saw the human spirit as immortal. It does not die and will find a home elsewhere. I remember being very impressed with the conversation because it explained how a person with such a ravaged body could remain so marvelously vital. I am sure that sense kept him going in some very painful times; and I suspect he believed his deeply ingrained integrity was something for the ages, not just this life. I don't think I have ever met anyone with such a profound belief in what the future will bring. I found the discussion virtually breath-taking, which is surprising for someone with my Agnostic orientations.

The experience with George confirmed something that I have believed for some time, namely that physical health and psychic health are two quite different categories. George was rare in his continued zest for living, despite his physical handicaps. One instance where George's psychic side triumphed over his physical occurred at one of the first Board meetings of the new George and Helen Hartzog Institute for the Parks. The conference venue was in Ashburn, Virginia, at least 30 miles from the Hartzog's McLean house. He was in extremely poor health, yet traveled to the meeting, and played a major role in its proceedings. It was very clear to me that the Hartzog spirit was alive and very well.

George Hartzog had tremendous inner resources, even as his health deteriorated. Frankly, I do not know what the elements of that spirit were; but they were manifested in his consistent good humor, his enthusiasm about life and its many events, his intellectual commitments and interests, and even a kind of unwarranted optimism.

Our discussions ranged over many subjects, but almost inevitably considerable time was spent on politics, much of it depressing because we were agreed on the inadequate performance of George W. Bush. Though Hartzog had been careful during his Park Service career to register as an Independent, he was, in fact, a deep-down FDR Democrat. He felt a great debt to Roosevelt because the Hartzog family had somehow survived the punishing Depression; and those experiences never allowed him to forget the needs of the less fortunate in the society. Beneath that gruff exterior,

George Hartzog was a "bleeding heart." We got along beautifully because our common experiences had led us to the same values and conclusions.

George was a great story-teller, and that persisted throughout his life. He was sparing, however, in the degree to which his tales dominated the conversation. He never descended into anecdotalism, a common malady of the aged and one for which George could have been most easily forgiven.

His love of books never diminished. When he was required to undergo dialysis, he reported to me that these sessions were the most awful periods of his life, nothing but excessive boredom. My query whether he thought books on tape would help him pass the time elicited an immediate and positive response. In the last days of his life he went to dialysis with a CD player and earphones, listening to David McCullough's *John Adams*, among other works. Even in his rapidly declining condition, he was taking great delight in these intellectual moments.

His unwarranted optimism surfaced in the rather constant effort to get his artificial leg into such shape that he could walk. The problems were immense, and I particularly recall his describing the difficulties in reestablishing a sense of balance. Almost to the end, I think George really believed he would walk again. It did not seem too much to expect of a spirit that had handled so many insurmountable obstacles in the past.

In addition to a set of strengths that made George Hartzog an extremely powerful person even as his health deteriorated, I observed other traits that persisted in old age and undoubtedly accounted for much of his success as a public leader.

Communication

It was fun to talk with George. The conversation was two-way, highly interactive. There was humility in his style; and it was easy for him to praise someone else. It seemed to me that he had immense personal confidence, and so it was no big deal to see the virtues in others as well. George was also never defensive. I interviewed him extensively on the accusations hurled at him for about five years after he had left the Park Service, and I found him totally objective about the whole ridiculous situation.

Warmth, Shows Emotion Easily, Caring, Tactile

On every one of my visits, there was a preliminary period when I was welcomed with extreme enthusiasm, told how much pleasure there was in seeing me, and finally received a big bear hug from the wheel chair. Sometimes there was considerable back-and-forth in our descriptions of how much we valued each other. While I was happy with my career, I always felt that George was going out of his way to make me feel good. He had done so much more than I had.

People-oriented

Much of his curiosity was handled, of course, by his voracious reading. But the interest extended beyond that. He was people-oriented. Whatever a person was doing held high interest for him. As an example, he had a great concern for our son, Jeff, who has been a lawyer in Washington for approximately 25 years. Jeff got career advice from George early in that period; and George monitored his successes with great approval. We almost never had a conversation when I was not asked to give a report on Jeff.

A Real Team: Helen and George

Though I have written briefly about Helen Hartzog as a caregiver in George's old age, there is far more to report on this marvelous marriage. It was an enduring love affair that lasted 61 years and was a source of great strength for George throughout his adult life. Indeed, he died the day before his 61st anniversary.

This is another area where I have felt a great kinship with George. My wife and I were married a few months later than the Hartzogs and have celebrated our 62nd anniversary. While the years do attest to a solid relationship, they are not the real story. I saw in the Hartzog relationship the same kind of caring and support I have experienced in my own marriage. For many men who achieve leadership positions, wives (and sometimes there are several of them) are just an asterisk in their biographies. Such men have made their way up the ladder as individuals, on a lonely journey. That is not the case with George Hartzog. He and Helen collaborated all the way. I appreciate fully how Helen made George's life richer and very likely more consequential.

George married Helen Carlson of Arlington, Massachusetts, in June 1947. She was a blonde, comely twenty-year-old then attending Boston University. She was already an accomplished pianist and had exhibited vocal talent, having appeared on a number of radio programs in the Boston area. The courtship had been a romantic one; and, from that time on, Helen had two loves, George and the National Park Service.

Married life began in Chicago, where the young couple found housing very difficult. George soon joined the Park Service, however, and thus began about 16 years of regular moves around the country. I calculate they transferred eight times between 1947 and 1963, when George returned to Washington to become the NPS Assistant Director. They were in D. C. for seven of those 16 years, however, so they were changing locations a great deal more frequently in the other years. These were not small moves. They involved Illinois, Texas, Colorado, Tennessee, and Missouri, as well as the District of Columbia.

Without doubt George's needs were dominant in the marriage. The two agreed completely on the importance of the National Parks, and so it was Helen's role to function as a facilitator, so that George could give himself as fully as possible to the parks. That included raising three children, accompanying George on major trips to Europe and Alaska among other places, cooking dinner on a moment's notice for a large number of people, hauling the kids to meet with Vice President Nixon at the Jefferson Park Memorial, and many other tasks too numerous to mention. George commented on her special capacities to represent him in this note:

> My absence from the NPS reception soon became obvious. Helen told me many people inquired where I was. She has an incomparable ability to smile, be gracious, say something and tell nothing.[11]

In a relationship as close as this one, it was inevitable that there were many moments of exploring issues and seeking answers. One such instance is found in George's book:

> I came home that night and Helen and I sat up until two o'clock in the morning talking about whether I should go ahead and leave or agree to accept the assistant secretaryship of Indian Affairs if the President approved it. Her question to me was, "Why did you come back to Washington, after you left in the first place?
> I said, "To be Director of the Park Service."
> She said, "That's right. And that's the job we both love. If you can't have that, tell them you don't want any." On that we went to bed.[12]

In my experiences with the couple, there are two long-standing memories. The first is the courtly manner in which George always referred to Helen. She was always "my bride." I do not remember a harsh word exchanged between the two of them. The second was Helen's persistently sunny and positive attitude. She was like her husband in this respect. Her first words to me were inevitably, "It's so good to see you." [Later, she might tell me she was dead tired.]

When Hartzog was well established as Director of the Park Service and keeping three secretaries busy, Helen's father died. As she said, he left her "a few pennies." She wanted to invest in real estate but knew nothing about it. Without telling anyone, she enrolled in a real estate course, completed it, then went to Richmond for the test, and passed that. She entered the real estate business when they were living in Arlington.

Helen was very good in real estate. She prospered and was able to make investments. It was she who acquired the highly valuable property on Chain Bridge Road in McLean, where they have lived for decades. Though I never talked with the Hartzogs about their finances, it is my impression that her real estate acumen contributed a great deal to the acquisition of substantial family assets.

She also had a great interest in antiques, and that led her to open a store in McLean that was quite successful. Today their colonial house is jam-packed with antiques. A number of years ago Helen made a trip south buying antiques. She had acquired such a collection that George cheerily drove a rental truck south to transport the acquisitions to McLean.

Leadership Attributes

My enumeration of George Hartzog's personal qualities has come from the many hours we spent together long after the conclusion of his Park Service career. In fact, of course, there is much more that can be said about his character, and more particularly about those attributes that made him a leader. In the cataloging that follows I have relied on what George has written about his experiences, what others have reported, and what I have personally observed. It is important to note that there are personality traits that rather uniformly equip a person for leadership responsibility regardless of the particular position occupied. Later, I will be concerned to delineate the characteristics that served George in his roles as an executive and as a manager.

Integrity

While we typically have many expectations of the leader, certainly none is more central than that there be an essential honesty not only of a personal sort but one which can be counted on to reflect the values of the community, no matter how large or small. In the Park Service this is critically important because of the nature of its mission, namely to protect and honor our national heritage. Commitment here becomes a synonym for integrity, where a person subjugates personal interest to the needs of the Park Service. Hartzog's clear and profound allegiance to the parks gave him credibility inside and outside their boundaries. He was seldom, if ever, accused of actions driven by personal ambition.

Courage

Another requirement of leadership is courage, for which there seem to be many synonyms: bravery, dauntlessness, gallantry, boldness, intrepidity, valor, fortitude, heroism. However I basically see courage as a willingness to take risks. Shortly after he became Director of the Park Service, Hartzog was faced with a seemingly impossible dilemma. It involved the Gateway Arch in St. Louis, in whose development he had earlier played such a major role. The Arch is defined as an Orthotropic structure, characterized by its verticality. This was the first such structure in the United States, its earlier usage having been in Europe.

The contractor for the Gateway Arch had never been involved in such an undertaking and came to the conclusion it would fall down. The designers, having European experience, were convinced otherwise. The issue went to the Secretary of Interior, who got advice from others in the Department that it would collapse. Hartzog realized that any real change in the Arch would essentially mean its end. While he was no engineer, Hartzog placed his faith in the designers, not in the construction people. The tense meeting with Interior Secretary Udall led to this proposal from Hartzog: "Continue the construction as planned. If the structure does fall, immediately fire Hartzog and blame him for everything." Udall accepted that bargain.[13] As we know, the two legs of the Arch fit beautifully. Joe Jensen, Hartzog's man on the project, wrote, "To lift the final section into place there had to be about a million pounds of pressure exerted on the two legs of the arch to allow the keystone to be placed..."[14] As Hartzog pointed out, it was Eero Saarinen's triumph in creating a memorial unique in the nation and the world. He reported further:

The theory of the orthotropic design is that the strength of the structure is greater than the sum of the strengths of the individual parts. The Arch consists of hundred of sheets of stainless and structural steel. Slowly and painfully each piece, different in size and shape, was fitted and welded into place. From the diversity of shapes, sizes, and materials the builders fabricated an arch that is, "Timeless, but of our time."[15]

Outside military conflict, it is hard to imagine how a person could have exhibited greater courage in a leadership role than Hartzog.

OPEN COMMUNICATION, LEVELING

While George Hartzog's capacity to communicate was established in many different settings and over a lifetime, there was an aspect that particularly pertains to effective leadership. It involves the capacity, indeed the courage, to level with people, to deal with an issue openly and straight forwardly. George had that kind of honesty. There are few, if any, who would say that Hartzog failed to level with them. When there was a problem with one of his superintendents, it was Hartzog who traveled to the office of the erring subordinate and candidly laid out the issues troubling the relationship. In doing so, George made sure that problems were fully aired and communications entirely open. It is a leadership style often advocated but seldom practiced.

AMBITION

An individual's goals and aspirations can be manifested in many ways. Often the desire is to reach positions that will advance personal goals and interests. In most organizations individuals can rather easily detect the motivations of leaders seeking gains for purely personal reasons. It is much rarer to encounter people who prize the leadership role for broader, social reasons. It is in this category that George Hartzog fits. Insofar as I know, Hartzog never had a greater ambition than to serve as Director of the Park Service. He left a much better paying job in St. Louis on Interior Secretary Udall's promise that he would be named Director. When Interior Secretary Rogers Morton urged Hartzog to move up to an Assistant Secretary's level, George spoke of his "druthers" to remain as head of the Park Service. After his departure from the Service, George settled into the practice of law. He never sought any other leadership role. I am sure this kind of commitment meant a lot to Park employees; virtually everyone knew he was on the side of the parks.

As I observed earlier, the behavior of an individual in a job is typically a consequence of the personal characteristics he/she brings to the position and the expectations directed to it by all those who might be affected. The mix between personality attributes and role expectations will vary according to circumstance. At the bottom of an organization we can expect that behavior will be governed primarily by role expectations, and job performance among individuals will be very similar. At the top of an organization, the signals are likely to be much more mixed, and individual traits will play a far greater part in determining outcomes. The reason for identifying the personality characteristics that very much attach to George Hartzog lies in the degree to which his own style established the way in which leadership was exercised in the Park Service. Even so, expectations from others exercised a constraint. Had he not been one of the five people recommended as his successor by Park Director Conrad Wirth,[16] Hartzog would have had far less credibility among his 13,000 employees and would have had to work much harder to establish his authority in the organization. Hartzog was aware of these forces. He would accept the position of Assistant Director only when Director Wirth specifically invited him to do so.

In the overall, however, George Hartzog must be regarded as a special individual, uniquely fitted to meet the challenge of leadership in the Park Service.

George B. Hartzog, Jr. the Executive

It is within this context that I characterize Hartzog as a model Federal executive. The conceptualization of such a leadership position is commonly attributed to Chester Barnard, himself a top business official, who published *The Functions of the Executive* in 1938. He rejected the idea that it was enough for leaders simply to "manage" the routines of the organization. Someone had to think more broadly, more comprehensively, and more creatively, both in terms of developing the inducements and understandings that would assure a committed membership and also in steering the enterprise in the treacherous waters that often put survival at risk.[17]

While he disagreed with Barnard in important ways on the nature of executive work, Harlan Cleveland was another source of support for the executive idea back in 1968. His well regarded book, *The Future Executive*, was often cited in our FEI literature because he also argued that there is a special role at the top for a few key leaders.[18] The imperative demanding such participation, in the Cleveland view, is complexity. He writes: "Executives are people who bring people together in organizations to make something happen. They live and work in the midst of events they help create. And the name of their game is complexity."[19]

A third authority to which we turned to certify the legitimacy of the executive role was the Committee on Executive Development. It issued a publication, *Top Management Development and Succession,* in 1968, which is perhaps most noteworthy for its dramatic justification for executive development: "To prepare managers more adequately for an uncertain future coping with job demands that have not been created."[20] Semantic confusion is caused, of course, by describing the objects of this kind of learning as managers, though the adjective "top" was often added. At another point the report emphasizes that these special people needed broadening, rather than increased specialization.

Most of the literature characterizes the executive as having a unique role, quite separate from the manager. The executive is perceived as being at the apex of the organization, concerned with the most critical issues relevant to its survival and long-term progress. Most significantly, the executive is viewed as having an overall grasp of the organization and its environment. That is why the concept of broadening is so important; and it suggests the reason why Cleveland pointed to complexity as its most central feature. Given these dimensions, it is understandable why executives were set apart from managers, who were seen as occupied primarily with the operations of organizations. Indeed, it was often contended that the executive should avoid the sin of becoming involved in management.

Whether George Hartzog was ever exposed to this kind of thinking, I do not know. But it is clear that is not the way in which he operated. He was an executive *and* a "hands-on" manager. He turned the theory on its head. As I will undertake to show, he brilliantly and emphatically discharged his responsibilities as the executive of a large and nationally significant organization. At the same time he had the energy and capacity to involve himself deeply in the management of the National Park Service. He showed that there is no incompatibility between the roles of executive and manager of an organization.[21]

How did he do it? First it should be recognized that most thinking about executives was premised on the expectation that rich management experience was a key requisite to elevation to the executive pinnacle. The problem was one of time. There was only so much an individual could do in ministering to the needs of an organization. The concept of specialization, a key structuring principle in most organizations, thus ordained that the executive confine himself/herself to that which seemed the unique obligation of the person at the top. Hartzog simply did not make this distinction; and he found the time to engage broadly in the activities of the Park Service, partly because of his individual traits and capacities and also because of the way he approached his management responsibilities. He was very careful about his choice of occasions for intervening in the internal operations of the Service. It was part of an overall management strategy which will receive greater attention later in this paper. Suffice it to say, his approach to managing the organization did accord him a certain freedom to range more widely in the organization than would be characteristic of many executives.

George Hartzog's position was that there was only one leader of the National Park Service, and it did not matter whether he was identified as director, executive, or manager. As it turned out, the willingness to take on the responsibility for the whole organization gave him a great deal of credibility.[22] When he declared that an action would be taken, everyone knew that the Park Service was committed. There would be no excuses that someone else had dropped the ball. This belief that promises would be kept was particularly important in Hartzog's relationships with the Congress, where he was most certainly performing an executive role. But it was as manager that he was able to assure Congressmen that commitments would be honored.

In describing Hartzog as an executive, it is important to emphasize again the values he brought to the situation. His love for the parks and the mission involved in their care and protection permeated his every act. Like any quality executive, he never forgot why his organization existed. In his oral history, Hartzog provides an excellent summary of what governed his executive behavior:

> The two books of which I am very proud are Ronnie Lee's book the *Family Tree*—it was the last book he wrote that was about the evolution of the National Park System—and Freeman Tilden's

Who Am I? I feel that the National Park's mission in life is to answer that question in our society, because we don't get it answered in the church. We don't get it answered in our political system. We don't get it answered in any of the other organizations of which we are members, because they're divisive in nature. Even the churches divide up into little sects and segments. As for our political system—if ever anybody wanted to know about its partisanship—I think that it's now at the worst stage I have ever witnessed in my eighty-five years.

None of those things tend to build a sense of community, which is so important to the freedom that we cherish as Americans, except in the National Park System, where you can't help, when you're standing alone in a redwood grove at Sequoia or Yosemite, that you know that you are a part of that system. And that was the theme of our [first] world conference: there's one web of life and you're a part of it. The web of life is in trouble and you can do something about it. It's the park system that knits that one web of life together and puts man at the center of it. That's what I think its ultimate value is all about, not baking in the sun or running ski mobiles, or Jet Skis, or anything like that.[23]

Within the Federal world of a George Hartzog, there are two highly critical forces with which people like him are likely to engage. One is the upper echelon of the Executive Branch, where, in this case, the Secretary of the Interior was Hartzog's direct boss and therefore his hierarchical superior. At a greater distance is the President of the United States, but its great visibility makes the Park Service a matter of continuing attention for the White House. While these Executive Branch relations (which can also involve attending to the egos of a wide variety of minions) must be maintained satisfactorily, the nation's legislative body, the Congress, may have an even more important say in the destiny of an organization like the Park Service.

George Hartzog was indeed a master in his capacity to deal with these often conflicting, frequently competitive elements in his environment. Because his accomplishments are so numerous and their specification is not required for this chapter, it is enough to stipulate his successes did occur and can be found in the many accounts of his service as NPS Director.

It is important, of course, to realize Hartzog's success did not come just from his good looks. He had a belief system, a set of personal traits, and a strategy that enabled him to meet some very great challenges. More than any other person I have known who was reared in the bureaucracy, Hartzog had a profound philosophical commitment to the kind of democracy found in the United States. While he vigorously participated in the process as a bureaucrat, it was Congress that had the legitimacy. He honored fully the decisions that were made; and he respected all of them, regardless of personal beliefs. He was the consummate democrat. His deep commitment to the Parks, along with his practical sense that he had to secure the necessary licenses and support for them, dictated that he engage the process fully.

An indication of the kind of energy Hartzog expended in the halls of Congress is revealed in this passage from his book: "When I returned to the National Park Service in 1963, I knew nine members of Congress. When I left at the end of 1972 I knew 300 and was on a 'howdyin' basis with most of the balance."[24] He also had a very clear picture of how he should relate to Congressmen:

> I tried never to take a Congressional member by surprise. That is the last thing a politician can stand.[25]

> Early on, I learned that the most important thing in the life of a member of Congress, whether in the House or Senate, is a constituent.[26]

> Except for the Chairman and ranking minority members of each committee and subcommittee, I did not make appointments. I simply stopped by the office, introduced myself to the receptionist and explained the purpose of my visit. If the Representative or Senator was available, I was usually introduced. If they were not in the office, I simply left my card and departed. Upon my return to my office, I always wrote a letter.[27]

Nor did Hartzog think of himself as the only official of the National Parks who should be paying regular visits to Congressmen. He asked each of his Park superintendents to call on the Representative for the district in which the park was situated and the two Senators. Again, it was not to make any demands but rather to pay a courtesy call. The superintendents were asked to leave a card and to declare to the receptionist that they wanted the Congressman to know they were available for any kind of service.[28] The inclusion of the superintendents in the Congressional rounds was, in many ways, a master stroke. The parks were important assets in local communities, and a positive association with them was important to many Congressmen.

During the interviews for his *Oral History*, Hartzog was asked this question: "What legislative achievement are you most proud of? Is there one piece of legislation that stands out in your mind?" In effect, the interviewer was asking Hartzog to reflect on his accomplishment as an executive. It was in his relationships with the Congress that he was called upon to discharge his most major executive responsibilities.

First noting that there were many successes with Congress in which he felt a great deal of pride, Hartzog continued, "If I were putting a priority on them, I would put the priority on the people side of it, the National Park Foundation, which today is a major source of funding for national parks and for program innovation, the Volunteers in Parks, without which the park system couldn't operate today. And, of course, the Alaska bill that preserved eighty million acres from state and Native selection in Alaska.[29]

While there were many achievements in his nearly nine years of service as Director that deserve reporting in these pages, considerable detail about many of these events is found in his book. It seems sufficient here to concentrate on the three that Hartzog identified as having special merit.

The National Park Foundation emerged early in his tenure as Director. What is notable is that the idea was not his. It was already in the files, and Hartzog revealed himself as free to use a good idea wherever it came from. It was former Director Wirth who had hired a financial consultant from Detroit and charged him with identifying a new means by which the Park Service could secure private funds for its public purposes. Hartzog describes the development of the Foundation in these terms:

> He [the financial consultant] came up with the idea that the trust fund board ought to be abolished and in lieu of it we ought to establish a regular foundation that would be managed by private trustees, and that would be the National Park Foundation. We didn't have any such thing as that.

That legislation was pending as a proposal, not as an introduced piece of legislation, but simply as a proposal in the Interior Department when I became director. It finally came to my attention, and I thought it was a brilliant idea. I talked with the committees and the committees agreed, so we introduced it and we passed it, and we were the first ones who had one of these National Park Foundations and it was the genesis, the groundbreaker, for seven more that followed for the Fish and Wildlife and Forest Service. All of the land management agencies, the Bureau of Land Management, wound up getting these foundations to support their programs. So that is the background on how we got the National Park Foundation.[30]

As he contemplated the needs of the Park Service, it became increasingly clear to Hartzog that needs for staff far outstripped the money available. There was a need for a "Corps of Volunteers," particularly in interpretation. With Secretary Udall's approval, Hartzog had his staff prepare proposed legislation for "Volunteers in the Parks (VIPS)." Before the proposal could be submitted to Congress, however, Lyndon Johnson announced that he would not run for another term. It was concluded that the new idea should be held over for a new Administration. Hartzog describes the process that followed:

> Soon after Hickel [the new Secretary of Interior] settled in, I produced the VIPS package. He embraced it enthusiastically. The Congress quickly passed the legislation.
> The new First Lady, Mrs. Nixon, inaugurated the program at Arlington House. We were off and running with what has become one of the most popular— and useful—of park programs.[31]

Clearly, Volunteers in the Parks was a tremendous innovation, and it is the vehicle which permits the Park Service, very much strapped for funds, to operate today. Virtually all the interpreters I have enjoyed for the last many years have been volunteers.

The significance of Volunteers in the Parks to the Service was emphasized by Helen Hartzog in a meeting we had in June, 2010. The Volunteers, she pointed out, now number 200,000 people, have their own organization, their own commitments, and their own plans to support the parks. They met in Washington at the Willard Hotel, and Helen reported that everything about their deliberations was truly impressive. As her gift to the group, she took them on a boat tour of the Potomac River. There was no doubt that Helen felt great pride in the organization, which she knew was another one of the many contributions George made to the Service.

While the National Park Foundation and the Volunteers for the Parks show the "people" side of the many Hartzog initiatives, Alaska is important for his contribution to the physical character of the parks. As he noted, the Alaska project ultimately brought 80 million acres under Park Service care.

Gaining this gigantic holding with state and Native American interests violently opposed was no easy process, and its accomplishment outlasted Hartzog's tenure in the Park Service. It was 1980 when this huge expansion occurred. But the events that provided the foundation for this major accomplishment reveal Hartzog the executive moving to ensure the preservation of one of America's greatest resources.

As he writes in his book, it was apparent early in Hartzog's tenure as Director that expansion of the parks in Alaska was not only a policy imperative but timely. Only four Alaskan areas had been included in the National Park system up to 1964. Yet for many years, some well before the Park Service was established, there was awareness of the natural and cultural treasures of Alaska. Numerous studies and reports had been completed; and, as Hartzog wrote, "Alaska was ripe for the taking."[32]

As was true with respect to any major policy action, everything depended on the Congress. In this case one Senator was key. He was Alan Bible of Nevada, and he held pivotal posts that controlled all legislation for the Park Service as well as the money that would be needed. Hartzog writes that he encountered Senator Bible in the halls of the old Senate Office building, where he was confronted by the words, "I ain't going to do it. I ain't going to do it!" When Hartzog asked what it was that the Senator wasn't going to do, he got this response: "I ain't a gonna make the whole United States a national park—not even for you."[33]

It was from this extremely discouraging departure point that Hartzog had to work toward a time when Senator Bible would not only accept but give real support to the expansion of the parks in Alaska. The means of persuasion was a trip to Alaska. In his discussions with Senator Bible, Hartzog discovered that the legislator had never been to Alaska and was expecting to rely heavily on the advice of the two Senators from Alaska. That was very bad news because the Alaskans' opposition to Park expansion was already well known.

After much cajoling, Senator Bible did agree to substitute a vacation already planned with old friends with a trip to Alaska. Hartzog writes: "Regional Director John Rutter and his intrepid crew organized the itinerary for a 'show me' trip such as none of us had ever experienced. By air, rail, boat and bus, we took the party all over the state to look at all of our major projects. Senator Bible and his friends were greatly impressed."[34]

That trip made Bible a believer. He asked Hartzog to provide him with the language needed for inclusion in the bill. The result was a provision that reserved 80 million acres, four million more than Hartzog proposed, largely for parks and wildlife preservation.[35] It appeared that this great expansion in Alaska would occur during the Hartzog tenure. For a variety of reasons, not unusual in the nation's political processes, it did not. It was nearly a decade later that the Alaska National Interest Lands Conservation Act of 1980 was passed. It added more than 43 million acres to the park system and more than 53 million acres to the national wildlife system, a total of 96 million acres. The concept was essentially that which George Hartzog had been developing since assuming the Directorship in 1964.[36] Several of the key figures involved in the 1980 legislation wrote to Hartzog in 1985:

> We equate you with the Redwoods, with the North Cascades, and—though few know this—with being the architect of the Alaska National Interest Land and Conservation Act. Together with Alan Bible and Scoop Jackson you wrote a chapter in the Park Service Book that reduces all other chapters—important as they are—to prologues and epilogues.[37]

While the Hartzog accomplishments with the Congress particularly deserve recognition, there are many other areas that also reveal his quality as an executive. I will mention only three.

The first is his ability to work with his boss. Hartzog served under three Secretaries of Interior, Stewart Udall, Walter Hickel, and Rogers Morton. They were very different people, two of them Republicans and one a Democrat. Yet it is evident that he was able to develop highly effective relations with each of them. Further, the association was of an executive nature.

Each was concerned with policy issues and left the management of the Park Service to Hartzog. Undoubtedly the closest collaboration was with Secretary Udall, which lasted for approximately five years. Udall's introduction to the Hartzog book provides an important insight on how he regarded his executive subordinate, included earlier in this volume.

Though it would seem managerial in many ways, Chester Barnard insisted that securing and maintaining a work force of high quality and commitment required executive involvement. Indeed, however the function is viewed, it is certainly true that George Hartzog brought major changes to the human composition of the Park Service.

As he pointed out, the Park Service had excluded more than half of the nation's population, essentially females and minorities, from contributing to the lofty enterprise of preserving and protecting the nation's parks. When he became Director, one woman was a superintendent; and she had the job because she had formerly been the secretary for a cabinet officer. There were no blacks in managerial positions of significance. And, if that were not enough, those who left the service were regarded as disloyal and not welcome back. It was clearly a tight, small society which had not yet recognized the importance of securing precious human resources from all segments of the society.

Hartzog's view of things was very different, and he attributes much of that to his southern background. Starting with his mother, he had known women who had kept families together and seen that they were fed during the Great Depression. In the small southern town of Walterboro, South Carolina, he learned that some of the most capable people in the community were black. As he observed in the interviews for the *Oral History*, one of the ablest people in town was a black electrician. George found the insistence that he enter by the back door absolutely abhorrent."That was repulsive," he commented. He felt his effort to secure major change in the human makeup of the Park Service had the full support of Secretary Udall and President Johnson."President Johnson's experience," he observed, "was very much like mine. We both were raised in the South."[38]

One of his earliest and boldest moves was to appoint a black Chief of the Park Police in Washington, D. C. It was the first time a black had headed a major police department in the United States.[39] The emergence of females in top leadership roles in the parks came more slowly, but roughly 30 years after Hartzog's directorship, his pioneering moves to open up the

Park Service had borne great fruit. Many females were Park Superintendents, and the Director who signed off on the Hartzog *Oral History* in 2006 was a woman, Mary A. Bomar, a careerist. She wrote: "His vision reflected the hopes and dreams of America, and his actions in personnel practices mirrored the initiatives of the 'Great Society.'"[40]

Hartzog the Manager

It is very difficult to separate the behaviors of George Hartzog as a manager from those as an executive. In any case it is apparent that the two were highly complementary. As I wrote earlier, Hartzog led the Park Service to high performance levels, an accomplishment well recognized in many companion organizations. [One report for the Office of Management and Budget in 1972 concluded that the Park Service was one of the five best managed agencies in the Federal government.][41]

Despite his high energy and numerous involvements, the fact was that Hartzog needed to develop a management strategy that called for 13,000 people to take major responsibility for the organization, limiting the leader's interventions to the real trouble spots or to occasions when the impact would be Service-wide. Within this context, Hartzog made it clear the system was hierarchical and he was the boss. He relied heavily on standard management tools in personnel and budget, as is clear in this quotation, in which there is also an expression of his sense of executive responsibility.

> The first thing I did when I came to Washington was I took control of the budget, personnel, and legislation with the explanation that I didn't care who approved the master plan. Nobody was getting any people or money until I approved the budget and made the personnel appointment. So the critical juncture of management is people and money, and then legislation, the foundation of both of them. You can't operate without money, and you can't achieve your objective of expanding the system without the Congress, because they set the public land policy of America. You don't. So you've got to involve them. I took legislation, budget, and personnel; they were my province. Then I delegated the rest of the operation to the deputy, associate, and assistant directors in the Park Service. Now, about that there are a lot of questions. Some of

them say it was a good job, and some of them say it was not done very well.[42]

It is significant that all the park superintendents were appointed directly by Hartzog. He reviewed the candidates, did the necessary interviewing, and determined how the various candidates would fit into his scheme of operation. It was his way of securing some assurance that people in leadership positions throughout the system were in some measure compatible with his style and orientation. There was also another way in which he made sure that the people coming up were his kind. Each Regional Director was required to submit to Hartzog annually a list of the five people in each organization with the greatest prospects for growth and advancement. Hartzog watched those people with great care and made sure that those meeting his standards were accorded development opportunities. At least in some degree, the Director, through his investment in key personnel decisions, built an organization in his own image.

He also had a great belief that money was the driving force in virtually all organization behavior. Thus he played a major role in determining how money was allocated among the many claimants in the Service. Further, he saw money as the key driver of change. Accordingly, he managed an arrangement with Congress where a small percentage of Park Service funds was reserved for use at the Director's discretion. That gave him the money to fund the changes he sought in the system. Here is how he explained things:

> The Congress went even further with me. While we were going in this period of expansion and innovation, they agreed that I could withhold from the appropriation an administrative reserve to solve immediate problems that came up. And I did. I withheld 5 percent of my appropriation, which I controlled. That's how I moved change in the National Park System. When I wanted something changed and called a superintendent and said, "I'd like it changed;' the first thing he did was look at it and say, "I don't have any money:' My response was, "If you would like to implement this change, tell me how much you think it will cost you and I will give you the money, and I will put it in your budget next year." And then I got change done. I got a lot of work done through that reserve. That money funded the innovative programs for serving

people, Summer in the Parks, Parks for All Seasons, Living History [program], all of those things that went to make our parks responsive to an urban environment came out of that reserve.[43]

A key concept, to which Hartzog was exposed in 1955, certainly seemed heretical in the Federal bureaucracy. The message was delivered to him at a Hotel Astor management seminar in New York City by Laurence Appley, the long-time President of the American Management Association. Appley had no use for staff assistants. The development of the "chief of staff" model, now found throughout the Federal bureaucracy, would certainly have been scorned by Appley.

Appley apparently had a great effect on Hartzog; and his adoption of Appley's ideas sent him apart from virtually everyone else in Washington. This is what Hartzog remembered Appley saying, more than 50 years later; Appley was telling about the time when he was Vice President of a large international oil company:

> As he related it to us, in his office there were two people, himself and his secretary. He pointed out that the reason was, "My managers in the field, when they had a problem, wanted to discuss it with me and not an assistant to me. And therefore I didn't need any staff." It was the tenor of that responsibility of a leader that I developed through that management program. I have a concept of management which I felt was pretty well grounded and was unique in terms of government service...[44]

Thus, *à la* Appley, there were no "assistants to" in National Park Service offices. Everyone had a clearly defined job in the organization. When the appointment was with the Director, the charismatic George Hartzog occupied center stage. The meeting was much more likely to deliver a personal experience, rather than a bureaucratic one. And it must have been, in many cases, a great surprise. It was so unlike Washington.

The Appley theory, of course, required a great many people doing their jobs well. While Hartzog had a great belief in the quality of Park Service staff, he was less sure that the organization was helping them realize their full potential. In order to play the role he envisaged for himself, Hartzog needed employees as enthused, as energized, and as inspired as he was.

Delegation was an important component of his management vocabulary, but it required a lot of trust and faith, not only in others but in himself.

One example of how the Hartzog mind operated involved an arrangement he made with R. T. Williams and me for some services from the Federal Executive Institute. [As it turned out, R. T. Williams played the major role.] Hartzog knew he was an extremely dominant figure in his relationships with his regional directors, who formed a key line of management in the Service. He saw them as passive, reluctant to challenge the boss, and unwilling to suggest new ideas. The obvious problem was that they felt they had no space in dealing with the boss. One answer was for Hartzog himself to engage in a retreat, to play a less active, engaged role in staff meetings. But that would have been very hard for him. He had to be George Hartzog, an exceedingly powerful individual. He concluded that the answer lay not with his changing but rather with transforming his subordinates.

His thought was to equalize power in these relationships by expanding that of his subordinates. In effect, he wanted Williams and me to create a somewhat subversive situation in which we would seek to empower the regional directors to confront and contend with their boss. Hartzog understood that the power relationships among individuals is not a zero-sum game. He did not see himself losing power in this process; rather the gains by the regional directors would constitute a gain for everyone.

You may wonder how the effort turned out. My recollection, which came largely from conversations with Williams and Hartzog and not from personal experience, is that the results were positive but not dramatic. People find it very hard to deal with a power figure who is moving generally in the right direction. I felt that this Hartzog initiative said a lot about him personally, namely that he had great personal confidence and also sufficient belief in his people that he could really feel it was possible to share power. In my experience such an attitude and its resulting action are very rare.

One of Hartzog's most dramatic moves to expand freedom and discretion throughout the Park Service was the abolition of all 56 of its administrative manuals. This was an act of rank heresy. The entire Federal establishment lives by its manuals. It is a means by which untold numbers of bureaucrats have avoided taking responsibility for their actions. It is the essence of managing by the book. On several occasions I have heard George Hartzog denounce this system of management. Even in 2006, roughly 40 years after he had departed the Director's position, he was still condemning this highly common bureaucratic pattern.

He found his first evidence of how unrealistic and ineffective the manuals were when he became Assistant Director of Rocky Mountain National Park. There he had to take an action on a concession and used a local form, rather than one in the manual. He knew what he was doing. He had written the manual, and he had no trouble deciding which one was superior. A copy of the document was submitted to regional headquarters. Not long after, there was a query from the Regional Director why the form in the manual had not been used. George explained the situation to the Park Superintendent, "Well, it's better than the one in the manual. I wrote the manual, so I know what I am talking about. If I had had this form, it would have been in the manual. So I recommend you put the manual in the trash, and that's what he [the Superintendent] did while I was standing there. We heard nothing further of the matter."[45]

In his *Oral History* Hartzog explains his feelings about the manuals very much as he criticized them to me:

> [The Park Service] had been an organization that was run by personalities and by administrative manuals. We had 56 of these books, and I was convinced that was the bottom line of why we couldn't bring about any change...I was convinced from what I was hearing that always we went back to those cotton-picking manuals.
>
> I asked the regional directors to look at the manuals. They agreed that many of them were out of date but said we should keep them because it insured uniformity, and that's when I became unhinged. I said, "You know, that happens to be the last thing I'm looking for. I want creativity, and innovation, and we'll get it my way, if we abolish them." And I abolished every one of them, thinking that never again would the Park Service be able to put them together because they wouldn't have that many people.
>
> The Park Service had become a bureaucratic organization hidebound by its books and its rules and regulations...we restored it [the old Park Service style] by abolishing handbooks, making superintendents responsible for management, saying to the employees what a satisfactory level of performance is, what the policies are

and they decide how to run the park on a day to day basis without having somebody in Washington write a book answering all of their unasked questions.[46]

The Hartzog approach to delegation made sense. Earlier he had developed six policies for the Park Service, which had been submitted to the Secretary of Interior and had been approved. Thus, there were clear guides for action but no instrumental instructions that might collide with sensible, policy-based judgments. Further, there were the unique Hartzog attributes of great personal confidence and trust in self, as well as trust in others to use themselves fully in the achievement of Park Service goals. The abolition of the manuals declared that Hartzog was willing to take risks far beyond the inclination and willingness of most Federal executives. It is apparent that the abolition of the manuals did no great harm to the Park Service, which continued to be regarded as one of the best managed of Federal agencies. There is, however, a question whether the lack of manuals functioned as a liberating force and promoted innovation and initiative. My impression is that George never got from the staff the kind of risk taking and new thinking he very much wanted.

Also, old habits do not die easily. Within five years of his departure, the manuals were back in full force. When Hartzog was commenting in 2006, there were 70, considerably more than the number he had abolished. Hartzog had this to say about their return: "Do you want to know the difference in the Park Service then and now? That's it! Now you're using a book to run the place, and back then we used people to run the place. I'm perfectly happy to have the record compared when we used people as opposed to when you use books."[47]

Delegation was highly critical to the Hartzog management strategy. While he was an energetic, full-throttle person, even he had his limitations. He could not engage in his broad executive functions, particularly his involvements with the Congress, and permit himself to be pinned down by operating minutiae. While the Hartzog interventions at times may have diminished enthusiasm for getting out in front, the Hartzog approach to delegation did work. He got a lot out of his people, and he was able to use his very considerable talents across a broad spectrum of activity.

Conclusion

It is hard to avoid the conclusion that George B. Hartzog, Jr. was a man possessing rare leadership talent. He set his own unique terms for discharging the significant responsibilities of the office. He is to be evaluated, then, not only for the great personal qualities he exhibited but also but also for the exciting, substantially different ways in which he constructed the role.

Certainly much credit must be given to Secretary of Interior Stewart Udall who, in a significant degree, "discovered" Hartzog. He deliberately sought out his new Director, who was then a young, well seasoned NPS veteran of 44 years of age. As Udall wrote, he wanted to make a "generational" change and thus to introduce a new edge into a well regarded but set in its ways Federal organization.[48] He could not have known how brilliant his choice was.

The appointment is noteworthy for another reason. It preserved the tradition that the NPS Director could be a careerist, selected from the ranks of experienced employees. For this both Udall and Hartzog deserve credit. When he assumed office in 1961 the Secretary did not assume he had the freedom to fire NPS Director Conrad Wirth. Though he probably already had the desire for a generational change, he acted only when Wirth announced his retirement to take effect in 1964. Hartzog was equally careful about observing the career tradition. He insisted on an orderly transition, in which he served as Assistant Director until Wirth's retirement took effect.[49]

The tradition of the NPS Directorship as a career position ended with the Nixon administration, which assumed control of the government in January, 1969. The change, though fairly subtle, occurred when Walter Hickel became Secretary of Interior. Up to that point, the Park Service had been regarded as a "closed" system, with only those in the NPS eligible for appointment to the Directorship. When Hickel came to power, however, the Hartzog tenure was regarded as ended. Hickel was free to make a new appointment, and presumably it could have come from outside the service. Hickel's reappointment of Hartzog, however, seemed to suggest things had not changed. A careerist was still in charge. But Hartzog owed his continuation in office to his skilled development of a policy agenda that appealed to Hickel, not to the fact that he was a careerist.

Although the White House was apparently unhappy with his continued presence, Hartzog served throughout Hickel's tenure.[50] When Hickel was fired, Rogers C. B. Morton, Hartzog's good friend, was named the Interior Secretary. Though Morton resisted the White House, the pressure was on. Hartzog had to go. Indeed, Hartzog reports in his book that a commonly identified condition of Morton's appointment was that he dismiss Hartzog.[51] The termination took effect December 31, 1972. That ended the career status of the NPS Director. The successor was Ron Walker, a member of Nixon's personal staff.

At the time George B. Hartzog was 52, undoubtedly ready for many more years of service. It certainly has to be regarded as a tragedy that a man of such quality and accomplishment would be removed from his leadership responsibilities at the peak of his career. It is not too much to believe that Hartzog might have continued until age 64, serving 20 years as NPS Director. Who knows what would have happened with that kind of stable leadership over two decades?

It seems clear that the antagonism toward Hartzog came directly from the President himself. And it seemed to be personal. Nixon was apparently no lover of the parks, but it is hard to imagine anyone feeling truly hostile toward them. Hartzog himself had had two contacts with Nixon when he was Vice President, and both were ceremonial. Neither seemed likely to generate intense feelings, positive or negative. Hartzog reported that Nixon refused to appear at the 100th anniversary of the establishment of Yellowstone in 1872 and sent his wife instead.[52] This may have suggested Nixon's passivity toward the parks; but, more importantly, it revealed where Hartzog stood. He was told he was not to appear with Mrs. Nixon in any picture-taking sessions.

Further, Hartzog found a passage in a memoir by Nixon's chief of staff, H. R. Haldeman, made at Camp David following the November, 1972 election: "Now on that, take that Park Service, they've been screwing us for four years. Rogers Morton won't get rid of the son of a bitch. But he's got to go."[53] It is still difficult to account for Nixon's truculent attitude. The occasional use of a boat dock at an island in Biscayne Bay seems as close to a triggering event as can be identified. Nixon and his friend Bebe Rebozo sometimes stopped there in the travels on the Bay. Rebozo had some interest in the property and kept his houseboat, from which his mother fished, there.[54] It was believed that Rebozo urged Nixon to fire Hartzog.[55]

Flimsy as the evidence was, Hartzog came to believe that his handling of the case, which he regarded as entirely proper and which included the provision of a special apartment for Nixon (which the President never used) was the cause of his removal.

What was the consequence of his seemingly arbitrary and unwarranted action? It deprived the Service of a man with rare leadership skills that were put entirely to the natural resource interests of the United States. As I have written earlier, George Hartzog was a man of great institutional, not personal, commitment. His ambitions were directed entirely toward the interests of the parks. He was summarily retired at age 52 and never again held public office. He wanted to devote his huge arsenal of capacities only to one mission, the protection and development of the parks.

There are few who could compete with Hartzog as an executive. If a particular responsibility of the top leader is to insure that an organization moves with the times, Hartzog certainly met the test. He employed the word relevance to explain his pursuit of change. As he said in his Oral History, "I think the word 'relevancy' is the word that occurs to me most frequently because unless the National Park System remains relevant to the changes in the society it is not going to last."[56]

He would have made Chester Barnard proud with the emphasis he placed on the human resources in the Park Service. Aside from the many ways that he assured their full utilization, it was he who opened up the system to the entire American population, giving both sexes and all races an opportunity for service. And the initiation of the Volunteers for Parks program gave a chance for 200,000 other Americans, some retired and others with extra time, to make a contribution to the parks.

Within the Federal establishment, he displayed remarkable executive skills. He worked with three different Secretaries of the Interior, each of very different political persuasions, comfortably and effectively. The relationship with Secretary Hinkel was perhaps most reflective of his executive talents. What convinced the former Governor of Alaska to keep him was the presentation of a policy agenda for the Park Service with which the Secretary could identify and enthusiastically support.

But it was Hartzog's ability to work with Congress that distinguished him from most Federal executives. He had a value system that honored the American democracy, and which was particularly alert to the role and significance of Congress. He never lost track of these moorings in his many dealings with Congress; and the result was a process of collaboration that few Federal executives have been able to achieve.

Added to all this, George B. Hartzog was a superb manager. His pattern of behavior broke with conventional theory that the management of operations is below the attention of the executive. For Hartzog that was most emphatically not the case. He was deeply involved in Park Service operations and declared himself its boss. As I have written above, this profound involvement in Park Service management endowed him with a level of credibility that few other Federal executives ever secure. Hartzog was able to engage in such an expansive role because he was a master of delegation. He determined where he had to intervene in the organization—personnel (particularly appointments), budget, legislation, and evaluation—to secure the influence he wanted in the organization. He had the kind of personal confidence that permitted him to cede important pieces of the action to others. Because he trusted himself, he was free to trust others.

Ironically, Hartzog was the kind of innovator Nixon said he wanted in government. The President brought in people like Roy Ashe and Fred Malek to shake up the government's management ranks. But he obviously never realized he had a gem in George Hartzog.

I have been an observer of the Washington scene for more than a half-century, having been an intern in the Federal government in1943, and I fail to remember a time when the bureaucracy was not littered with "assistant tos," whose purpose always seemed to be to attend to the needs of a higher-up. The problem has become even more severe in recent times as "chiefs of staff" have proliferated throughout the departments and agencies. Even more than was the case in the past, this new crop of high level officials are occupied only with the support and service to a particular boss.

Thus George Hartzog's strong commitment to the Lawrence Appley doctrine that there should be no assistants in the executive suite has particular relevance. In the Park Service Hartzog insisted that everyone have a job description specifying responsibility to the system, not to an individual in it. He declared that he served the parks and insisted that everyone see things similarly. It was refreshingly different from the way in which most of the bureaucracies in Washington were conceived and operated. And it would be even more heretical today.

The anger Hartzog expressed toward the Park Service manuals involved much more than a procedural issue. His abolition of the 56 manuals existing at the time reflected a major philosophical position on how the Service would be managed. As I have noted above, Hartzog believed that the

Park Service had to be a changing organization. It had to be relevant. That required room for innovation and experiment. The manuals carried the message, however, that there was an approved and proper way to carry out virtually ever function of the system. There was no place for innovation, and things were made worse because Hartzog had first-hand knowledge of the ways in which many of the manuals were developed. He knew they did not even reflect best practice at the time.

I believe that Hartzog instinctively recognized innovation was the key to the development of a learning organization. If people felt they had to go through an established drill in which there would be not learning, the chances for institutional change and personal development would drop essentially to zero. It was important manuals not be seen as the last word.

Finally, there was the issue of accountability. With resort to the manuals, officials could avoid responsibility. They could argue they simply went by the book. What Hartzog wanted were people who felt free to think freshly. He authoritatively set goals for the Service, approved by the Secretary of the Interior, and the idea was to work creatively within these terms. Again, this is very different from the culture common to the Federal bureaucracy, where manuals and procedural mandates dominate most action.

What is interesting is that Hartzog's abolition of the manuals did not lead to organizational collapse. While they may not have gone as far as Hartzog would have liked and may have leaned on procedures already in their heads, members of the Park Service made sure that the system performed effectively. Here is how Hartzog summarized the experience:

> I thought we wound up with a much more creative organization than we started with. I say it was because I abolished 56 volumes of handbooks, and I had those three little policy manuals, and that was it. If you didn't find it there, you were supposed to have a solution in your head, not that somebody was going to write it up from Washington.[57]

It is ironic that this major change, which had the effect of freeing up the organization to be far more innovative, lasted less than five years. At the time Hartzog was recording his *Oral History*, the number of manuals had risen to 70. Hartzog reflected on his situation with exasperation, "Well, I wasn't gone five years before they had written up to 70 volumes of them.

Do you want to know the difference in the Park Service then and now? That's it! Now you are using a book to run the place, and back then we used people to run the place. I am perfectly happy to have the record compared when we used people as opposed to when you used books."[58]

When the whole Hartzog record is laid out, it is difficult to determine what really stands out about the man. Certainly his out-size personality, with its attendant charisma, is of major significance. But, in the last analysis, here was one smart man who was humble enough to realize there was always more he could learn and use.

Notes

1. Frank P. Sherwood, editor. *The Early Years of the Federal Executive Institute*. (New York and Bloomington, Ind. : iUniverse, Inc., 2010), 573 pp.
2. George B. Hartzog, Jr., *Battling for the National Parks* (Mt. Kisko, NY. : Moyer Bell, 1988), 16.
3. *Loc. cit.*
4. *Ibid.*, 20.
5. *Ibid.*, 16.
6. *Ibid.*, 16–17.
7. *Ibid.*, 21.
8. *Ibid.*, 19.
9. *Loc. cit.*
10. *Ibid.*, 21.
11. *Ibid.*, 77.
12. *Ibid.*, 246.
13. *Ibid.*, 53–5.
14. *Ibid.*, 56.
15. *Ibid.*, 57.
16. Conrad L. Wirth, *Parks, Politics, and the People* (Norman, Oklahoma: University of Oklahoma Press, 1980), 301.
17. Chester I. Barnard, *The Functions of the Executive*. (Cambridge: Harvard University Press, 1938).
18 Harlan Cleveland, *The Future Executive: A Guide for Tomorrow's Managers*. (New York: Harper and Row, Publishers, 1972).
19. Cleveland, 7.
20. Committee for Economic Development, *Top Management Development and Succession*. (New York, 1968), Supplementary Paper No. 27, 46.
21. George B. Hartzog, Jr., et al., *Oral History Interview with George B. Hartzog, Jr., Director, National Park Service, 1964–1972* (National Park Service, Dept. of the Interior, 2007).

    In a "Foreword" to the *Oral History*, Robert M. Utley, a former Chief Historian of the National Park Service, provided these characterizations of George Hartzog: "he not only managed he ruled"; "a workaholic who drove the staff at his pace"; "deeply caring, friendly, and sentimental with everyone"; "nearly tyrannical in his demands for superior performance"; "entertained a broad vision of what the national parks should be and pursued his vision ruthlessly"; "possessed political cunning, insight and mastery almost nonexistent among Federal heads"; "led the largest expansion of the National Park Service in history. During his nine year tenure, the system grew by 72 units, totaling 2.7 million acres." (ii–iv)

22. George often said, "I can delegate authority but not responsibility."
23. Hartzog et al., *Oral History*, 43.
24. The following excerpt from the *Oral History* suggests that the Park Service can survive without White House support as long as there is a person like George Hartzog at the helm. He observed that the Nixon Administration was unalterably opposed to the expansion of the parks. But the decision about expansion was not fully Nixon's.

    Hartzog commented, "I never had a lot to do with him (Nixon) because Nixon's senior staff never went to the parks. Nixon, I think, went to the Grand Teton National Park once, unlike Kennedy, who made a tour of the national parks when he became President.

    "So there was not a lot of direct contact. But there was enough that they knew who I was, and primarily where we had contact the most was on the Hill, because the Nixon administration wanted no Park legislation. Of course, coming off the Johnson administration, I had a tidal wave of legislation in the Congress, and, as you see in the record, we passed almost as much in the Nixon administration's four years as we did in the Johnson five years, because the tide was coming in and there was literally nothing they could do to stop it…my relations on the Hill were perhaps better then the President's in terms of getting legislation through. Nixon reciprocated by never having a park signing ceremony. He never had one, whereas with President Johnson, his staff would set them up before I even got the bill passed." (32)

25. Hartzog, 137.
26. *Ibid.*, 122.
27. *Ibid.*, 120.
28. *Ibid.*, 118.
29. Hartzog et al., 34.
30. *Ibid.*, 58.
31. Hartzog, 96.
32. *Ibid.*, 205.
33. *Ibid.*, 203.
34. *Ibid.*, 213.
35. *Ibid.*, 213.
36. *Ibid.*, 220.
37. *Ibid.*, 221.
38. Hartzog et al., 15.
39. *Ibid.*, xiii.
40. *Ibid.*, i.
41. Hartzog, 111.
42. Hartzog et al., 10.

43. *Ibid.*, 39.
44. *Ibid.*, 3.
45. *Ibid.*, 8.
46. *Ibid.*, 14.
47. *Loc. cit.*
48. Hartzog, xiii.
51. *Ibid.*, 245.
52. *Ibid.*, 239–41.
53. The quotation is from H. R. Haldeman, with Joseph Di Mona, *Ends of Power*. (New York: Times Books, 1978). Cited in Hartzog, 239.
54. *Ibid.*, 238.
55. *Ibid.*, 248.
56. Hartzog et. al, 59.
57. *Ibid.*, 61.
58. *Ibid.*, 14.

Notes on Contributors

Lawrence R. Allen, Clemson University, currently serves as the Dean of the College of Health, Education and Human Development, a position he holds after over seven years as Head of the Department of Parks, Recreation and Tourism Management. He is a Fellow with Academy of Leisure Sciences, and in 1995, served as the President of the Academy. In 1996, he was elected to the American Academy of Park and Recreation Administration. He has a very strong commitment to professional practice in park, recreation and tourism services and has served on various boards of directors, and state and national committees. He presently serves on the Board of Directors for the George B., Jr. and Helen C. Hartzog Institute for Parks, and he has been active with a consortium of universities advising the National Park Service on leadership development for the 21st Century.

At the end of December 1999, **Barry Mackintosh** retired from the National Park Service after serving 17 years as bureau historian. He began his NPS career in 1965 when he was hired as a historian at Fort Caroline National Memorial in Florida. In 1968, after two years in the U. S. Army, Mr. Mackintosh began work as a historian at Booker T. Washington National Monument in Virginia. A year later, he was assigned to Fort Frederica National Monument in Georgia. Between 1970 and 1978, he worked for the History Division in Washington, D. C. For four years, between 1978 and 1982, he served as regional historian in the National Capital Region of NPS. In 1982, he became burea historian. The Library of Congress catalogue lists 13 works by Mr. Mackintosh, covering histories of the national park system and administrative histories of national parks and NPS programs. He received his B. A. degree from Tufts University and his M. A. degree from the University of Maryland.

Frank P. Sherwood is an Emeritus Professor of Public Administration, Askew School of Public Administration and Policy, Florida State University. His last assignment at FSU was as the Jerry Collins Eminent Scholar in Public Administration (1991–1995). He retired in1995. He has authored, co-authored, or edited 15 books, covering a wide range of subjects generally in the area of government and its management. Sherwood has authored or co-authored more than 50 papers which have appeared in scholarly journals, as well as more than 25 essays in various books. His academic assignments have included Director of the School of Public Administration, University of Southern California; Director of the Federal Executive Institute, Charlottesville, Virginia; Director, Washington Public Affairs Cemter, University of Southern California; and Chair, Department of Public Administration, Florida State University. He is a Past President of the American Society for Public Administration,1973–74; and is a Fellow of the National Academy of Public Administration, since 1969. Sherwood has homes in Tallahassee, Florida, and in Annapolis, Maryland, where he resides with his wife Frances. They have two children, Jeffrey Kirk, an attorney in Washington, D. C., and Robin Ann, a financial planner, in Connecticut.

As Secretary of the Interior from 1961–1969, **Stewart L. Udall** made his mark as an environmental and cultural visionary. In addition to acting as the facilitator of the National Park System's expansion in the 1960s, Udall was instrumental in the creation of the National Endowments of the Arts and the Humanities and spurred the establishment of several of America's most treasured performing arts facilities. Additionally, Udall's *The Quiet Crisis*, published in 1963, is numbered among the key works to have triggered the environmental movement. Unsurprisingly, Udall's tenure as Secretary saw the implementation of key environmental legislation, including the Wilderness Act, the Water Quality Act, and the Wild and Scenic Rivers Act. The former Secretary died on March 20, 2010.